"Wish I knew what to say..."

When you're camping with family or friends, especially if you're a camp counselor or leader, there are times when the beauty of God's creation calls for a psalm of praise ... when the awesome grandeur of nature sets a mood of worship.

... under rolling clouds in a sky without horizons

... beneath a shady tree, feeling thankful

... in a sudden, violent summer shower

... when you glimpse the top of the mountain through trees

... beside a roaring, dancing stream

... watching a chipmunk, darting bullet-fast

... in the warmth of campfire fellowship

... even wondering why God made ants and mosquitoes!

Here are devotions to help you make the most of these priceless moments.

CAMP DEVOTIONS

Dick and Yvonne Messner

David C. Cook Publishing Co.
850 NORTH GROVE AVENUE • ELGIN, IL 60120
In Canada: David C. Cook Publishing (Canada) Ltd., Weston, Ontario M9L 1T4

To
Our Lord and Savior
Jesus Christ
Creator and Maintainer
of the Great Outdoors

CAMP DEVOTIONS
Copyright © 1974 David C. Cook Publishing Co.

All rights reserved. Except for brief excerpts for review purposes, no part of this book may be reproduced or used in any form or by any means—electronic or mechanical, including photocopying, recording, or information storage and retrieval systems—without written permission from the publisher.

David C. Cook Publishing Co., Elgin, IL 60120

Printed in the United States of America
Library of Congress Catalog Number: 74-75540

ISBN: 0-912692-41-3

Introduction

BIBLE TEACHING for children in camp should be different from teaching at home or in church classes. It should take advantage of camp experiences, to introduce Biblical insights at the "teachable moments" in each exciting day.

That is why the authors have felt a need for a devotional guide which uses the "encyclopedia" approach. Devotional themes should be chosen which center on a favorite spot in God's outdoors, a spirit-moving moment, people in camp, or natural objects and living things.

We sometimes like to call our way of selecting devotional themes "the smorgasbord method of Bible study." Pick a spot, a time, or an animal you have just seen in the woods. Using this volume, you'll be able to find a related Bible passage which can be the basis for an inspiring meditation.

In *Chapter I* we have included 45 of such short talks, in outline form. You'll notice that these are grouped in eight series.

Chapter II keys hundreds of additional Bible passages to camp and nature themes.

Chapter III is an invitation to use your imagination and tie your devotions into the camp schedule, with dramatic punch.

Jesus never spoke without using illustrations, and his visual aids were divinely created. He spoke of the flowers, the trees, water and fish, the mountains, the sea, fire, wind, rain, and God's creatures big and small.

Our Lord spent much of his time on the trail. He roamed the land bringing the message of God's new Kingdom. His feet grew dusty and sore. He rested on the hillsides, ate on the beaches, sailed on the waters of the Holy Land. Nature was His amphitheater.

Nature is especially fitted for teaching us of God. As Psalm 19 tells us of one part of creation: "The heavens declare the glory of God; and the firmament sheweth his handywork." Paul wrote to the Romans, "the invisible things of him [are] understood by the things that are made."

Our little Marlene was helping us clean up the yard recently. She suddenly looked up and said, "What does Jesus do all day?" Well, for one thing, we told her, Jesus not only created our world, but He is busy making sure that it is maintained. The sun has to shine, and the rains must come to keep the earth clean and fresh. The birds need food, and the earth must continue to rotate properly, and so on.

I Corinthians 8: 6 reads, "To us there is but one God, the Father, *of whom* are all things." God the Father was the Master Architect who conceived the plan of creation. He was the one who drew the plans.

Then our text goes on to say, ". . . and one Lord Jesus Christ, *by whom* are all things." Jesus Christ did the creating. He was the Master Builder. John reminds us that without Him nothing was made (John 1: 3).

And Jesus Christ is not only the Creator, He is the Maintainer of this magnificent universe. Paul says that "by him all things consist" (Colossians 1: 17). The word "consist" literally means to "hang together." Jesus Christ could be thought of as the "glue" that holds this universe together.

But what about the Holy Spirit? Didn't He have a part in creation? He certainly did. Job 26: 13 reads, "By his spirit he hath garnished the heavens." The beauty of creation is a testimony to the Spirit of Life.

May the triune God make Himself known to your campers or family through your use of *Camp Devotions*.

Winona Lake, Indiana   YVONNE MESSNER
RICHARD G. MESSNER

TABLE OF CONTENTS

Devotional Outlines
1. *Sky* — 11
2. *Water* — 21
3. *Field* — 31
4. *Wind* — 47
5. *Fire* — 57
6. *Weather* — 67
7. *Mountain* — 77
8. *Life* — 91

Seed Thoughts
1. *Camping* — 105
2. *Animals* — 106
3. *Insects* — 109
4. *Plants* — 110
5. *Birds* — 113
6. *Trees* — 115

Dramatic Devotionals
1. *The Beach* — 121
2. *The Hillside* — 125

I
Devotional Guide

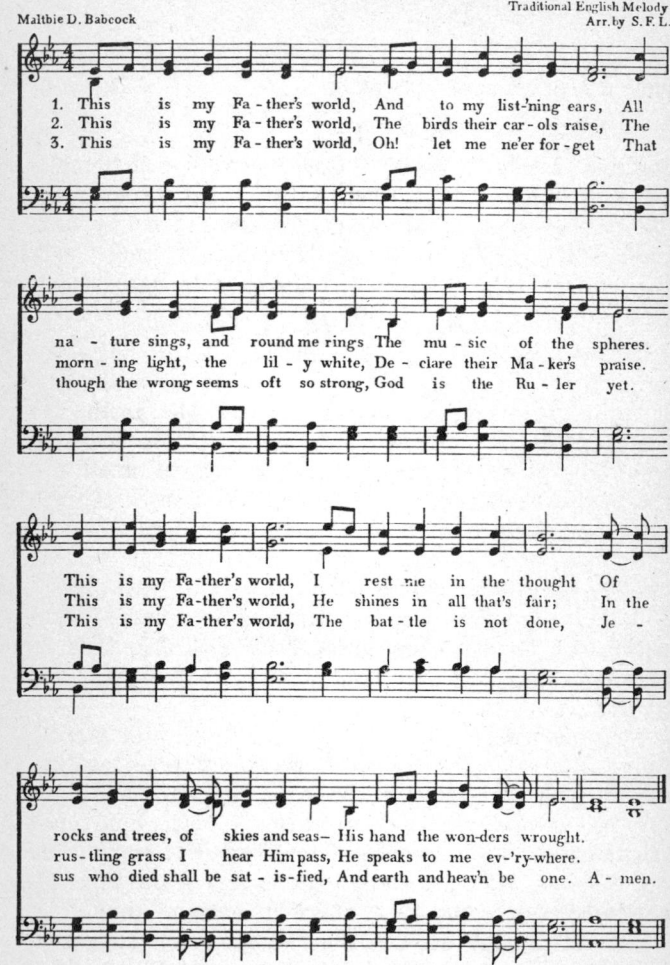

Sky

PICK A SPOT: Under blue skies

PICK A LESSON: *God's Home*

GOD SAYS (Acts 7: 48-50): "God doesn't live in temples made by human hands. 'The heaven is my throne,' says the Lord through his prophets, 'and earth is my footstool. What kind of home could *you* build [me]?' asks the Lord. 'Would I stay in it? Didn't I make both heaven and earth?'" (*The Living Bible,* a paraphrased version.)

THINK ABOUT THIS: Look up at the sky! Do you see God's home? Look to the east: perhaps you see the rising sun. Is God's home there? Look to the west, the north, and the south. Look at all the beautiful creation of God—His trees, His plants, His flowers, His creatures small and great! Is God's home among them? The answer to each question is yes! *All of it* is God's home.

Picture God sitting on His throne in the highest Heaven—above the clouds, above the stars. Now picture Him reaching down to earth, with His feet planted right near you. "O Lord, how great Thou art!" There is no building that could ever hold Him! He is too great and too marvelous for us to imagine!

No wonder that He says, "For lo, I am with you always." And, "Where two or three are gathered together in my name, there am I in the midst of them." For He is present everywhere in His created world. Your best friend can be with you most of the time, but no one—no one but God, that is—can be with you all of the time. He can be anywhere and everywhere at the same time.

On the Mount of Transfiguration, Peter suggested building a home for Our Lord, Moses, and Elijah. Such a foolish question received no answer!

So God does not live in buildings made by man, not even a gigantic Astrodome. Where does He live? The world is His home. But He has another special place in this world where He desires to dwell. And that is deep in the heart of each Christian. Your body can be the temple or dwelling place of the Holy Spirit (I Corinthians 3: 16). Belief in the atoning work of Christ on the cross is all that's necessary.

Outdoors, we are in the home God has created for *us*. There we can fellowship with Him.

Another home for us is being prepared in Heaven. It took God six days to create the earth; He has been preparing Heaven ever since!

ASK YOURSELF: Is Christ living in me? As a guest in God's house, have I ever thanked Him? Is any problem of life too big for Him? Am I looking forward to being with Him in my heavenly home?

PRAY ALONE TO GOD.

PRAY ALOUD: Dear God, thank You for letting me enjoy Your home today. Thank You for furnishing it so beautifully. Thank You for offering Your Son as my sinless substitute. I look forward to entering Your heavenly home someday. Let me share Your love today.

Sky

PICK A SPOT: Under blue skies

PICK A LESSON: *Windows of Heaven*

GOD SAYS (Malachi 3: 8-10): "Will a man rob God? Surely not! And yet you have robbed me. 'What do you mean [you say]? When did we ever rob you?' You have robbed me of the tithes and offerings due to me. And so the awesome curse of God is cursing you, for your whole nation has been robbing me. Bring all the tithes into the storehouse so that there will be food enough in my Temple; if you do, I will open up the windows of heaven for you and pour out a blessing so great you won't have room enough to take it in!" (*The Living Bible*).

THINK ABOUT THIS: Picture God stepping into your presence in human form, right now. He steps up to you and says, "Stand up, I want to have a word with you."

"Uh-hum. Yes, Sir!"

"I have a question to ask you. Why have you robbed Me?"

"Robbed You? Why, I didn't rob You! I wouldn't do that to anybody!"

"Haven't I given you life and breath? Haven't I given you the clothes you wear, the food you eat, and a place to sleep? Don't I provide for you, every day?"

"Why, yes, Sir, You do, and I appreciate that."

"But what have you ever given Me?"

"Well, I try to bring my money to Sunday school each week."

"Is that what I asked for? You'll remember that I have asked you to bring one tenth of all you possess to Me. And after that, an offering of love for all I've done for you. Bring them to the church, so that there will be plenty of money for the church to care for the sick and homeless, and those who desperately need help. Look up to the heavens now—see those clouds. In that one large cloud, you'll see a large opening. It's like a large window. I could cause rain to fall. It would cover you in moments, and you would run for cover. Or, I could cause thick flurries of snowflakes to fall. Don't you see? In the same way, I will pour out great blessings on you—so great that you won't be able to contain them. Your joy will be full! All I ask is that you obey Me."

"Yes, Sir, I see now. By keeping back what doesn't really belong to me, I have robbed You."

ASK YOURSELF: How often have I robbed God? How much do I owe Him? Do I want the windows of Heaven to open on me; to fill my world with great and bountiful blessings?

PRAY ALONE TO GOD.

PRAY ALOUD: Forgive me for not showing my thankfulness to You in a tangible way. Help me to give back to You the rightful part that belongs to You. And then let me do more for those who really need it. Shower me with blessings from the windows of Heaven.

Sky

PICK A TIME: A starry night

PICK A LESSON: *Merely Man*

WHAT GOD SAYS (Psalms 8: 3—9: 2): "When I look up into the night skies and see the work of your fingers—the moon and the stars you have made—I cannot understand how you can bother with mere puny man, to pay any attention to him! And yet you [created] him only a little lower than the angels, and placed a crown of glory and honor upon his head. You have put him in charge of everything you made; everything is put under his authority: all sheep and oxen, and wild animals too, the birds and . . . all the life in the sea. O Jehovah, our Lord, the majesty and glory of your name fills the earth. O Lord, I will praise you with all my heart, and tell everyone about the marvelous things you do. I will be glad, yes, filled with joy because of you. I will sing your praises, O Lord God above all gods" (*The Living Bible*).

THINK ABOUT THIS: Look up and see the vast Milky Way galaxy, the system of stars to which our sun belongs. There are billions of stars up there. With the 200-inch mirror in a telescope at Mount Palomar, you can see 100 million galaxies much like ours, with billions of stars in each. Do you realize that God has made each one of these?

No one yet has been able to measure the breadth and depth of the heavens. We know that it would take a plane traveling 1000 miles an hour nine days to reach the moon, or three years to Venus, the planet nearest the earth. But it would take three million years at that speed to reach the nearest star!

Is it any wonder that David the Psalmist says, "God, I can't understand how You can bother with mere man!"

God has made each one of us in His image. He has placed a crown of glory and honor upon my head and yours. He has put us in charge of all the birds, fish, and tame and wild animals of the world. He has put the fear of man in them, and we are to have authority over each one.

When we view the moon (the closest heavenly body) and the stars (the farthest creations of Heaven), what a magnificent thought to know that God cared enough for you and me, a mere pinpoint in His sights, to give us such honor and power.

As a powerful man is to a tiny ant, so God must be to us! Yet He loves us with an everlasting love! He could crush out our lives with the touch of His finger, but He chooses to guide us with His hand.

Yes, God is so great, and we are so puny! But God is so *good*, and we should sing His praises back toward the skies.

ASK YOURSELF: When I consider the heavens and how great You are, how can I do less than to give You my best and live for You completely?

PRAY ALONE TO GOD.

PRAY ALOUD: Dear God, thank You for making each star and each planet and hanging it in space for me to see. Thank You for making me and giving me such a high place in Your sight. Make me worthy of Your love in my loving and caring for others. Let me tell everyone about all the marvelous things You do.

Sky

PICK A TIME: A starry night

PICK A LESSON: *God's Maintenance Work*

GOD SAYS (Psalm 104: 19-24): "He assigned the moon to mark the months, and the sun to mark the days. He sends the night and darkness, when all the forest folk come out. Then the young lions roar for their food, but they are dependent on the Lord. At dawn they slink back into their dens to rest, and men go off to work until the evening shadows fall again. O Lord, what a variety you have made! And in wisdom you have made them all! The earth is full of your riches" (*LB*).

THINK ABOUT THIS: Scientists tell us that it takes approximately one month for the moon to orbit around the earth—sometimes longer, sometimes less. Thus from the beginning of recorded time, man has used the moon as a guide to mark the months of the year.

It takes the earth just 24 hours to rotate on its axis. When the sun is turned away from the earth, the moon is visible. Therefore we have day and night, marking one complete day.

God is not only the Creator of this marvelous universe, He is also the Sustainer of it. Have you ever wondered what God does all day? Perhaps you will picture Him sitting on His heavenly throne watching us busy little creatures.

Did you ever consider the monumental task He has of maintaining the universe? (What would happen if *you* didn't keep *your* things neat and clean, never washed, or never picked up after a meal?) God makes sure that the moon and the sun rotate on schedule. He tells His creatures of the forest to come out at night for food, while man is asleep. He provides enough food for them to eat. He tells them where to find it, and how much they should eat. Do the animals depend on God more than we do?

God made the thousands of varieties of trees and plants and animals. He made the powder-blue sky to go with the deep blue sea, and the bright green grass. He made the gorgeous shades of gold, brown, and red on the autumn leaves as they blend into a blazing wave of beauty. He made the majestic mountains and covered them with a cloud of red and white in the morning sunlight. He made the velvet red rose, the blazing blue morning glories, the fields of dotted daisies, the tiny wild violets, and the burnt orange fields of tiger lilies. There is no end of the beauty of the earth. How rich we are!

God did this all by means of Wisdom—not just an attribute, but by Wisdom personified: His Son, Jesus Christ (I Corinthians 1: 24; John 1: 3, 10, 14).

ASK YOURSELF: Have I ever fully appreciated what God does in maintaining this universe for my enjoyment? Have I ever thanked Him for all the beauty that I see each day? Have I trusted Him fully to provide my every need just as He does for the animals? Is it any wonder why I enjoy being in the outdoors so much?

PRAY ALONE TO GOD.

PRAY ALOUD: Thank You for the beauty of the earth, for Your constant care of it, and of me. May I trust You completely today for my every need. Thank You, Jesus, for making the world such a truly beautiful place to live in. Help me to do my part to keep it that way.

Sky

PICK A SPOT: Under a red sky

PICK A LESSON: *Signs of the Times*

GOD SAYS (Matthew 16: 1-4): "One day the Pharisees and Sadducees came to test Jesus' claim of being the Messiah by asking him to show them some great demonstrations in the skies. He replied, 'You are good at reading the weather signs of the skies—red sky tonight means fair weather tomorrow; red sky in the morning means foul weather all day—but you can't read the obvious signs of the times! This evil, unbelieving nation is asking for some strange sign in the heavens, but no further proof will be given except the miracle that happened to Jonah.' Then Jesus walked out on them" (*LB*).

THINK ABOUT THIS: Have you heard these sayings?

"Evening gray and morning red/sets the rain upon your head/but evening red and morning gray/sends the sun upon its way."

"Red skies at night/sailors' delight/red skies in the morning/sailors take warning."

Now you know that these sayings were first found in the Word of God. Look at the sky around you. Can you predict what kind of day it will be today, or tomorrow?

Skeptics of Jesus' day were taunting Him and asking Him to do some miracle in the sky to prove that He really was the Son of God. But God says in His Word that He doesn't perform miracles just for foolish tests or for the whims of men.

This should be a warning to us, not to "put out the fleece" or to test God about everything. He has given us good minds and we should use them whenever we can.

Isn't it interesting that Jesus was speaking here to a group of people much like unbelievers or skeptics today. He says it was an evil, unbelieving nation. We have only to listen to a "Billy Graham" shout from the pulpit, "Repent, ask God to forgive your sins, and turn from your wicked ways," to know that people today are not any different.

Jesus told them that there is only one sign that they shall have, and that is of the prophet Jonah. Jesus was saying to them that what happened to Jonah was already a miraculous sign—why should they look any further?

The scriptures say, "Even as Jonah was three days and three nights in the belly of the great fish, so shall the Son of Man be three days and three nights in the heart of the earth" (Matthew 12: 39, paraphrase). Jesus went to the depths of suffering for you and for me at Calvary.

ASK YOURSELF: When I look into the sky and see the signs of the weather, do I think of the sign of the water below, that of Jonah? Do I think often of what Christ did for me when He died on Calvary? What have I done for Him?

PRAY ALONE TO GOD.

PRAY ALOUD: God, thank You for the signs in the sky, for the sign of Jonah, and for the sign of Christ at Calvary. Make me a signpost for Christ wherever I go in this evil and unbelieving nation.

Water

PICK A SPOT: Near a tree by the water

PICK A LESSON: *A Good Man*

GOD SAYS (Psalm 1: 1-3): "Oh, the joys of those who do not follow evil men's advice, who do not hang around with sinners, scoffing at the things of God: But they delight in doing everything God wants them to, and day and night are always meditating on his laws and thinking about ways to follow him more closely. They are like trees along a river bank bearing luscious fruit each season without fail. Their leaves shall never wither, and all they do shall prosper" (*LB*).

THINK ABOUT THIS: God uses the illustration of a tree: tall, beautiful, strong, full of foliage, rooted deep by the water's edge.

This "good" man is God's man, one who truly loves God with all his heart. Jesus said, "Who is a good man? There is none good, but God!" So the good man does not walk with those who ignore God. He does not spend time with those who ridicule the things of God.

But he spends time each day, and often, mulling over in his mind the things He has read in God's Word, the Bible. In this way he is like a tree, standing firm against the pressures of earth, his inner being (or roots) reaching deep into the water of the Word for bountiful spiritual blessings. This will make him strong against all the forces of evil—the storms of life, such as trials and temptations, and the strong winds of opposition from those who hate God.

As a result of putting God first and drinking continually at His fountain, God says that we will never die, and whatever we do will prosper.

Joyce Kilmer wrote:

> I think that I shall never see
> A poem lovely as a tree.
> A tree whose hungry mouth is prest
> Against the earth's sweet flowing breast;
> A tree that looks at God all day
> And lifts her leafy arms to pray;
> A tree that may in summer wear
> A nest of robins in her hair;
> Upon whose bosom snow has lain;
> Who intimately lives with rain.
> Poems are made by fools like me,
> But only God can make a tree.

God made the mighty oaks and giant redwoods; He also made the fragile birch and tender saplings. As the storms of time beat upon the giant trees, they have weathered many a storm, and their roots are deep and standing firm. When the rains lash the tender, tiny trees, they bend with the pressure—but if rooted deep, they bounce back to grow straight and tall. The old, old trees, and some young ones which have dried up, with shallow roots will soon die, then be struck down with a bolt of lightning or a strong wind.

Every time you look at a tree today and marvel at its beauty and strength, think of your life.

ASK YOURSELF: Am I strong enough to withstand the pressures of life? How deep are my spiritual roots? Do I want to be really successful? What must I do?

PRAY ALONE TO GOD.

PRAY ALOUD: Dear Lord, may I be wholly Yours. Fill me with the refreshing water of the Word each hour in this day. Make my life full and fruitful for Your honor and glory. Let me learn from this tree the lesson of the good and righteous man.

Water

PICK A SPOT: Near a body of water

PICK A LESSON: *Don't Be Afraid*

GOD SAYS (Mark 6: 47-51): "During the night, as the disciples in their boat were out in the middle of the lake, and [Jesus] was alone on land, he saw that they were in serious trouble, rowing hard and struggling against the wind and waves. About three o'clock in the morning he walked out to them on the water. He started past them, but when they saw something walking along beside them they screamed in terror, thinking it was a ghost. . . . He spoke to them at once. 'It's all right,' he said. 'It is I! Don't be afraid.' Then he climbed into the boat and the wind stopped!" (*LB*).

THINK ABOUT THIS: The odorless, colorless currents of air, in the form of a mighty wind, slap against the water—at times whipping up furious waves and whitecaps. Often boats are dashed to pieces against rocky river beds; sometimes lives are lost. Imagine yourself seated in a small craft in the midst of a tempestuous sea of water—not in sunlight but in the dead of night.

Perhaps you started out on a nice boat trip about dusk. Enthralled with the glowing sunset, rippling waves, and lapping of the water against the boat, you didn't notice the dark clouds forming to the west. When you finally turned around to head back to camp, the sun was fast fading. Within a few minutes it was all dark. The storm clouds rolled, and the waves rocked the boat. You weren't going to make it. "What will I do?" you shouted to whoever might be listening.

It was much the same spot the disciples found themselves in. Pulling hard on the oars, they struggled against the high waves, to little avail. Then suddenly they saw a white figure walking past them on the water, and they screamed in terror. Sounds like a Halloween ghost story! No, it's a true story. That figure was Jesus! He came to them, walking on the water. Immediately sensing their fear, He spoke. "Don't be afraid, it's Me!" He climbed in the boat and the wind stopped.

How often we let the terrors of life—a bad dream, a frightening thought, a hopeless situation—overtake us completely. We want to scream. We are overcome with emotional and physical terror. We think there is no way out, no one to help us.

But Jesus Christ is standing there beside us on the water, or wherever we are, saying, "Don't be afraid, I'm here!" Then He climbs in beside us, and the fears are gone. He is there to comfort and to guide us. He can stop the wind and waves in your life. He can solve every problem.

ASK YOURSELF: Do the problems of life loom as giant waves, against which I have no power? Do I let Jesus Christ calm all my fears? Am I going to trust Him today for everything?

PRAY ALONE TO GOD.

PRAY ALOUD: Dear God, You know I'm only human. You know that I let the things of this life bring fear into my heart. Come into the boat of my life today. Be my Navigator all the rest of the way, through all the storms of life. I want to put my trust in You completely!

Water

PICK A SPOT: Beside a large body of water

PICK A LESSON: *Depend Upon God*

GOD SAYS (Psalm 104: 25-29): "There before me lies the mighty ocean, teeming with life of every kind, both great and small. And look! See the ships! And over there, the whale you made to play in the sea. Every one of these depends on you to give [him] daily food. You supply it, and they gather it. You open wide your hand to feed them and they are satisfied with all your bountiful provision. But if you turn away from them, then all is lost. And when you gather up their breath, they die and turn again to dust. Then you send your Spirit, and new life is born to replenish all the living of the earth. Praise God forever! How he must rejoice in all his work!" (*LB*).

THINK ABOUT THIS: Perhaps you stand beside a river, a small lake, or even a pond. But the same ideas you have just read are true about this body of water. When you think of the thousands of kinds of water creatures, too numerous to count, you realize the monumental task that God is performing.

How often have you bent down and opened your hand to feed one of God's creatures? Perhaps it was at a children's zoo, at a roadside park, or in your own backyard. You might even have a pool of fish which you feed each morning. Since they are captive you must care for them.

But each one of God's water creatures depends upon Him for food each day. Think of the thousands of bodies of water the world around! Think of the millions of fish and sea creatures there are! God is interested in the life of each one. He provides its every need.

What if God should turn His back? What would happen? The same thing that would happen if you stopped feeding a pet fish or pet animal. Each would die!

We often forget to take care of pets daily, if we don't really love them. But God doesn't forget. And if God cares enough to feed each sea creature each day, how much more does He care for you?

Remember that God said, "Let us make man in our image. . . . So God created man in his own image, in the image of God created he him; male and female created he them" (Genesis 1: 26, 27). When a child is born into your family, how much do you love him? Could it be that you love the baby because it resembles Mom or Dad, or you—is in your image? Each of us, whether we realize it or not, resembles God. We are made in His image.

Fish die, and so do people. But the Holy Spirit brings new life to the earth in the form of newborn babies.

If you let God's care for His creatures sink into your understanding, you will soon be swelling up with praise to the Savior. You will want to shout, "Thank You, Lord" for giving us life and caring for us day by day. To think, that I was made in the image of God!

ASK YOURSELF: How much do I love Him who created me? How much do I depend upon Him for my daily needs? How much do I praise Him for all His great works in my behalf?

PRAY ALONE TO GOD.

PRAY ALOUD: Dear God, thank You for the fish in the sea. Thank You for caring for me. Thank You for letting me know that you see each step that I take. Thank You, God, for loving me so.

Water

PICK A SPOT: Beside quietly flowing waters

PICK A LESSON: *Everything I Need*

GOD SAYS (Psalm 23: 1, 2): "Because the Lord is my Shepherd, I have everything I need! He lets me rest in the meadow grass and leads me beside the quiet streams. He restores my failing health. He helps me do what honors him the most" (*LB*).

THINK ABOUT THIS: Looking down into the rippling brook or softly flowing stream, you feel a sense of strength—and yes, calmness. The Lord who made this body of water is saying, "I am your strength; now rest in me." He made the fields on a thousand hills. He made the green grass to grow, and now He says, "Come and rest, I have everything you need."

Everything I need? Well, let's see. As I venture into the outdoors, I need a *guide,* one who "knows the ropes." Could God be that Guide? "In all thy ways acknowledge him, and he shall direct thy paths" (Proverbs 3: 6).

I need *food and drink.* Could God supply that? He says, "I am the bread of life: he that cometh to me shall never hunger" (John 6: 35).

I need *rest.* "Come unto me, all ye that labour and are heavy laden, and I will give you rest" (Matthew 11: 28).

I need *companionship.* "I will never leave thee, nor forsake thee" (Hebrews 13: 5).

I need *hope.* The prospect of living with God forever makes this life "bearable." "For God so loved the world [each one of us], that he gave his only begotten Son, that whosoever believeth in him should not perish, but have everlasting life" (John 3: 16).

I guess we'd have to say that David was right that the Lord can supply everything we need. And the best part is, it's not just for now but for eternity. A story is told of a fire in a barn where sheep were. After frantically herding the sheep out of the barn, the leader sheep became confused and ran back into the barn. All the herd followed and perished in the flames. *In contrast,* our Shepherd leads us out into life and never fails us. He keeps us safe, and deserves our trust.

ASK YOURSELF: Is the Lord my Shepherd? Am I ready to follow Him through all the fiery trials of life? Do I depend upon Him for everything I need? Or do I choose the path of complaining and worrying!

PRAY ALONE TO GOD.

PRAY ALOUD: Dear God, I will follow You faithfully in every passing day. My tomorrows are all known to You. I trust that You will lead me all the way.

Water

PICK A SPOT: Near a well, pump, or fountain

PICK A LESSON: *Love Story*

GOD SAYS (Exodus 2: 15-17): "Moses ran away into the land of Midian. As he was sitting there beside a well, seven girls who were daughters of the priest of Midian came to draw water and fill the water troughs for their father's flocks. But the shepherds chased the girls away. Moses then came to their aid and rescued them from the shepherds and watered their flocks" (*LB*).

THINK ABOUT THIS: At each campsite there is a central place where you can draw water for cooking, for drinking, and for washing dishes. It's usually in the center of the camp or next to the washrooms. It's important for a group to find out upon arrival where the water supply is. Often it's there you meet other campers and have fellowship with them.

In the days of Moses, the local well was a gathering place for friends. All the teenage girls would go there to draw water for their households, hoping to meet some interesting young men. (You'll remember the story of Jacob's servant finding Rachel at the well.)

It doesn't take too much imagination to visualize what happened on the day Moses arrived at the well in Midian after his exhausting trip across the desert, running from the Egyptians. He was sitting down taking a drink when he saw seven lovely girls, daughters of a preacher, coming to draw water for their father's sheep. The shepherds milling around at the well probably nudged each other and said, "Hey, look what's coming!" "What dolls!" "I got my eye on the redhead!"

When the girls came closer, the shepherds no doubt went to meet them and began teasing them. Irritated, they tried to ignore this. But their annoyance grew when they were prevented from getting water. Finally Moses chased the shepherds away. Then he drew water for the girls' flock.

In exchange for helping the girls, Moses was invited to supper. Then he was invited to live with the family. Finally, he married Jethro's oldest daughter, Zipporah.

I suppose the moral of the story would be: Trust in God's will; look to Him for all your needs; be kind to those around you. God will give you bountiful blessings.

ASK YOURSELF: Am I running away from something? Am I willing to stop and rest, and drink from the well of God's Word?

PRAY ALONE TO GOD.

PRAY ALOUD: Dear God, thank You for supplying water, both natural and spiritual, continually for my needs. Keep me in the center of Your will for my life, that I may receive blessings from Your hand.

Field

PICK A SPOT: A field

PICK A LESSON: *Buried Treasure*

GOD SAYS (Matthew 13: 44): "The kingdom of heaven is like unto treasure hid in a field; the which when a man hath found, he hideth, and for joy thereof goeth and selleth all that he hath, and buyeth that field."

THINK ABOUT THIS: How much fun it is to go on a treasure hunt at camp. There's nothing more exciting than looking for and finding buried treasure! Mystery, suspense, intrigue, and danger stalk the brave souls who venture to look for it. And who wouldn't buy a piece of land if they secretly knew it held a treasure?

A common understanding of this parable is that Jesus Christ is the hidden treasure, and that men should be willing to sell all they have in order to obtain His salvation. Variations of this view make the treasure to be the Gospel, or membership in God's Kingdom. But the sinner, of course, has nothing with which to *buy* salvation. Nor is he supposed to hide the Good News after obtaining it, as in the parable.

Since Jesus is talking directly to His disciples, a reasonable interpretation makes this parable an explanation of their place in the Kingdom. God's people are called His *treasure* in several Old Testament passages.

The field is the world. God's people were chosen by Him out of all the world to be a witness to the Truth in the midst of idolatry. They have been His treasure, hidden among the unbelieving people of the world.

According to this interesting interpretation, Jesus Christ is the One who sold all that He had in order to purchase His people. By doing so at Calvary, He obtained full ownership of the treasure. Now He owns the field [the world] with the treasure [His people] hidden in it. They are hidden there for safekeeping.

In the meantime, God is still dealing with mankind—calling out a people which is very precious in His sight.

ASK YOURSELF: Am I one of those who are precious in His sight? If Jesus Christ gave all that He had for me, am I willing to bring forth fruit and serve Him?

PRAY ALONE TO GOD.

PRAY ALOUD: Dear God, thank You for this story of hidden treasure. I want to be something special for You. Let me bring forth the fruits of love, joy, peace, patience, gentleness, faithfulness, and self-control (Galatians 5: 22, 23) in relationship to all those around me.

Closing Song

RUTH ODOR

DORRNANCE ISAAC B. WOODBURY 1819-1858

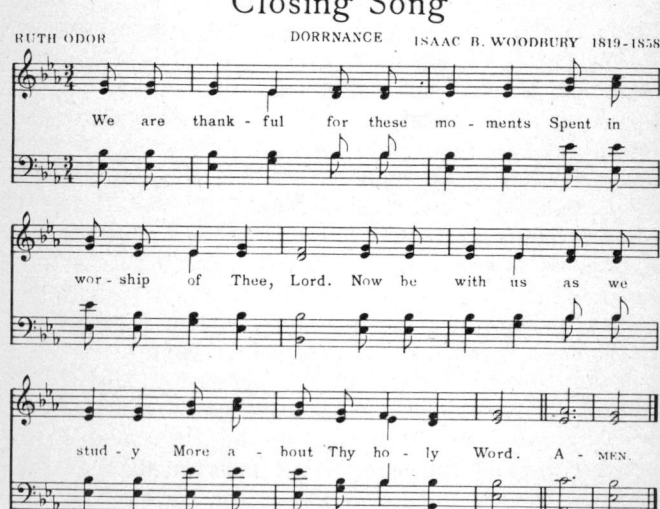

We are thankful for these moments Spent in worship of Thee, Lord. Now be with us as we study More about Thy holy Word. A-MEN.

Words © David C. Cook Publishing Co., 1967.

Field

PICK A SPOT: A field

PICK A LESSON: *Lazy Fellow*

GOD SAYS (Proverbs 24: 30-34): "I walked by the field of a certain lazy fellow and saw that it was overgrown with thorns, and covered with weeds; and its walls were broken down. Then, as I looked, I learned this lesson: 'A little extra sleep, A little more slumber, A little folding of the hands to rest' means that poverty will break in upon you suddenly like a robber, and violently like a bandit" (*LB*).

THINK ABOUT THIS: There are fields, and there are fields! Some are well kept and flourishing, producing lots of grain or vegetables. Others are unkempt, weedy, and run down! You can tell a lot about a farmer when you look at the fields that he keeps.

Looking at that field of the lazy fellow in Proverbs, we can learn a lesson. The "lazy fellow" represents one who doesn't really care about anything. When you talk to him about something he ought to do, he says, "I don't care!"

"You ought to be careful of your language, Son!"/"I don't care!"

"Watch the way you hold your fork; be a gentleman at the table."/"I don't want to be a gentleman!"

"Why not try to be nice to your sister sometimes?"/"I don't care about her."

"Don't you think you should try to make it to prayer meeting this week?"/"I don't care about prayer meeting!"

"I understand that you took something from the store the other day without paying for it."/"Everybody rips off stuff; they don't care, and I don't care!"

The thorns, weeds, and broken-down walls in the story speak of the wrong things we do. The sleeping, slumbering, and resting speak to us of letting these misdeeds go and go, until suddenly we wake up and find we have robbed ourselves of everything we held dear.

Suddenly, nobody cares about you! No one will lend you any more money. No one wants you for a friend. No one cares whether you have enough clothes, or food. No one cares whether you live or die. Then it may be too late!

But the old adage, "Better late than never!" applies even here. Better to wake up and get going, even if you're a bit late. Care a little! God cares about you!

ASK YOURSELF: Have I been in a trance? Can I see what I have done by thinking always of myself, and seldom of others? Can I stop my slumber? Will God forgive me?

PRAY ALONE TO GOD.

PRAY ALOUD: Forgive me for not caring enough for You, for not caring for others! Help me turn around! Keep me spiritually alive and active through loving You and loving others.

Field

PICK A SPOT: A field where thistles grow

PICK A LESSON: *Jesus As a Farmer*

GOD SAYS (Matthew 13: 24-30): "Here is another illustration Jesus used: 'The Kingdom of Heaven is like a farmer sowing good seed in his field; but one night as he slept, his enemy came and sowed thistles among the wheat. When the crop began to grow, the thistles grew too. The farmer's men came and told him, "Sir, the field where you planted that choice seed is full of thistles! . . . Shall we pull out the thistles?"

"' "No," he replied. "You'll hurt the wheat if you do. Let both grow together until the harvest, and I will tell the reapers to sort out the thistles and burn them, and put the wheat in the barn"'" (*LB*).

THINK ABOUT THIS: Are you puzzled? Well, the disciples were, and they asked Jesus what the parable meant. Here is His answer:

I am the farmer who sows that good seed. The *field* is the *world*, and the *good seed* represents the people who believe in *God*. The *thistles* are the people belonging to *Satan*. The *enemy* who sowed the thistles among the wheat is the *Devil*. The *harvest* is the *end of the world*, and the *reapers* are the *angels*.

Now that you have the key to the mystery of the story, you can tell it this way: The good grains of wheat, God's people, are sown by God and told to live in the world. Satan plants his host, the thistles, in among God's people in this world. These thistles grow big and fast, and like to choke out the good seed.

Ever touch a thorn, or try to pull one out? Ouch! It hurts! Even thick gloves can't keep the pricks out. Ungodly people are often like that. They get into positions of power and authority and they like to work against God's people. They sometimes use words sharp as thorns.

At the end of history, Jesus will come for His own. Then the thistles will be removed. The good plants will be taken into the joyful presence of the Lord.

ASK YOURSELF: Am I like the good stalk of wheat that grows tall and straight and can be used for God? Or am I like the thistle growing stout and thorny, choking those around me by my sharp comments and criticism?

PRAY ALONE TO GOD.

PRAY ALOUD: Plant my feet on solid ground. Let me grow tall and straight for You. Help me bear the attacks of temptation upon my life. I look forward to being with You for eternity.

Field

PICK A SPOT: A farmer's field

PICK A LESSON: *The Harvest Is Ready*

GOD SAYS (John 4: 34-38): In answer to a question about the food Jesus had, He explained: My nourishment is doing the will of God and finishing His work. Do you think the work of harvesting won't begin until the summer ends, four months from now? Look around you! Fields of human souls are ripening all around us, and are ready now for reaping. The reapers will be paid good wages and will be gathering souls into the granaries of Heaven! What joys await both sower and reaper. (It is often true that one sows and someone else reaps. I sent you to reap where you hadn't sown; others did the work, and you received the harvest.) (Paraphrased.)

THINK ABOUT THIS: Every time we see a field of golden, flowing wheat, a vast cornfield, or a farmer's orchard just ready for picking, we are reminded of this story Jesus told His disciples.

His first point was that spiritual food is far more important than physical food. With the vital interest in getting enough food to eat, the disciples may have found it difficult to think along these lines. But the hunger of the body is for this life only. The significance of spiritual food and life is eternal.

Today in our "overweight" nation, many people are overconcerned with rich foods and underconcerned with spiritual life. Christians should be like Daniel and his friends, who would not eat the idol-worshiping king's rich food. They preferred to fast and be fed in spirit by their heavenly Father.

Jesus' second point was that while the disciples were thinking so much about food, people around them could be dying without faith in Him. Many of these people had heard the Gospel taught by Him or by His disciples, but were still waiting to be claimed for the Kingdom.

What Jesus was saying to His disciples then, He says now to you and me: "John, you spoke to Mary the other day about your love for Me, but she was not ready to come to Me for forgiveness of her sins and for eternal life. So Tom, you go now and talk to her. She is ready to accept Me now."

In a farmer's field some will plant the seeds, some will weed and cultivate, and still others may come to reap the harvest. So it is with the Gospel of Christ. Some will plant, by giving a personal word of love for God. Others will water with a verse of Scripture or by showing Christian concern at just the right time. Still others will ask a soul to accept Christ and be ready to bring that soul into the courtyard of Heaven.

God honors the planter, the cultivator, and the reaper. You can be one of these today. Speak of Him to those you meet.

ASK YOURSELF: Am I ready to be used by God? Have I accepted Jesus as my Savior and become His disciple? If so, am I willing to share the wonderful Good News with others?

PRAY ALONE TO GOD.

PRAY ALOUD: Father, thank You for sending someone to harvest my soul at the proper time in my life. May I today be a planter or a reaper for You. Let me care more for things above than things here below. I will love You more today than I ever have before.

Field

PICK A SPOT: A field or path

PICK A LESSON: *The Good Earth*

GOD SAYS (Luke 8: 5-8): "A farmer went out to his field to sow grain. As he scattered the seed on the ground, some of it fell on a footpath and was trampled on; and the birds came and ate it as it lay exposed. Other seed fell on shallow soil with rock beneath. This seed began to grow, but soon withered and died for lack of moisture. Other seed landed in thistle patches, and the young grain stalks were soon choked out. Still other fell on fertile soil; this seed grew and produced a crop one hundred times as large as [had been] planted" (*LB*).

THINK ABOUT THIS: Jesus interrupts His story at this point to say, "If anyone has listening ears, use them now!"

The *seed* is God's message to men. It is the Gospel of God's love in sending His Son to die for our sin. By faith in Him we can have eternal life.

The *hard path* where some of the seed fell represents the hard hearts of some who hear God's Word. Satan steals the Word away before it can sprout.

The *stony ground* probably represents unbelievers who may even enjoy listening to sermons; somehow the message never really gets through to them—doesn't take root. They halfway understand that the message is true, but soon lose interest.

The *seed in a patch of thorns* represents those who listen and make a beginning at believing God's Word, but whose fledgling faith afterwards is choked out by worry or riches—the abundance of responsibilities and pleasures in life.

The *good soil* represents honest, good-hearted people. They listen to God's words and cling to them. Their lives bear spiritual fruit.

Around your campsite, you are bound to see these four types: a hard path, a stony site, thorny ground, and good, rich soil. Let them remind you of the hearts of men.

ASK YOURSELF: What kind of ground is *my* heart like? Do I refuse to believe in God? Do I forget God as soon as people kid me about my faith? Or am I just too busy with all of my own problems to grow up in the Christian life?

PRAY ALONE TO GOD.

PRAY ALOUD: God, let my heart be good, rich soil. May I cling to You and Your Word. Let the beauty of Christ be seen in me, as in a rose among thorns.

Field

PICK AN OBJECT: A vine and its branches

PICK A LESSON: *Bearing Fruit*

GOD SAYS (John 15: 1-8): I am the true Vine, and my Father is the Gardener. Every branch of mine that doesn't bear fruit, He removes. Each branch that bears fruit, He will prune so that it will bear *more* fruit. . . . Just as the branch can't bear fruit unless it is attached to the vine, you can't bear fruit unless you hold on to Me. I am the Vine, you are the branches. In Me you can bear much fruit. . . . That will honor and please My Father. (Paraphrased.)

THINK ABOUT THIS: Look at the vine, strong and sturdy! Where are its roots? Deep in the earth. Its branches reach out and produce rich fruit.

The Vine is Christ; the branches are believers in Christ, whose main food comes from the Vine.

Cut a branch from your vine! What will happen now? Yes, it will die. Perhaps you will burn it. A person cannot live spiritually apart from Jesus Christ.

God, the Gardener, must prune the branches by cutting them back from time to time. So He sends trials and problems our way—but gives us comfort and the grace to endure them. It hurts each time, but in the end we are stronger for having experienced pain. God must continually discipline those He loves, to make them spiritually stronger and enthusiastic about the things of God. (Hebrews 12: 7; Revelation 3: 19.)

Fruit bearers are those who love God, obey Him, and live for Him each day. They display in their lives the fruits of the Spirit—love, joy, peace, patience, kindness, faithfulness, gentleness, and self-control (Galatians 5: 22, 23, *The Living Bible*).

There are three levels of a person's ability to bear fruit. The first level is *without fruit,* a Christian who fails. The second level is *fruitful;* living in Christ, and growing. The third level is *bearing much fruit.* Now you are wholly living for Him, being pruned continually but suffering in silence—praising God in all the circumstances of your life, and growing in the gifts of the Spirit.

God promises to help you grow, if you will cling to His Vine.

ASK YOURSELF: At which level am I? If I know Him, how much fruit am I bearing? In what spiritual characteristics (Galatians 5: 22, 23) am I weakest? Am I willing to live for Him completely?

PRAY TO GOD ALONE.

PRAY ALOUD: Dear God, help me to cling to Jesus. I trust You for an abundant life through Him. I commit myself completely to You, and will obey Your Word even during the hard times.

Field

PICK A SPOT: *Where wild lilies grow*

PICK A LESSON: *Stop Worrying*

GOD SAYS (Matthew 6: 28-34): Why worry about your clothes? Look at the field lilies! They don't worry about theirs. Yet King Solomon in all his glory was not clothed as beautifully as they. And if God cares so wonderfully for flowers that are here today and gone tomorrow, won't He care for you?

So don't worry so much about having enough food and clothing. Why be like unbelievers? They take pride in such things and are deeply concerned about them. But your heavenly Father already knows perfectly well that you need them, and He will give you what you need if you give Him first place in your life.

Don't be worried about tomorrow. God will take care of your tomorrow, too. Live one day at a time. (Paraphrased.)

THINK ABOUT THIS: Many flowers are called lilies. In many countries in early spring, the ground is carpeted with the lilies' brilliant blossoms. The most common lily in our country is the beautiful, belled "Lily of the valley." It grows in patches, with large leaves protecting each slender stalk. Its fragrance is so sweet that perfume is made from its delicate flowers.

In the summer, you are apt to find wild tiger lilies up to three feet tall along the roadside or covering a large field. Slightly smaller than the white Easter lily, they are a deep orange—truly colorful against the mass of greenery surrounding them.

Jesus was speaking to a crowd near Gennesaret, in a district noted for its masses of colorful flowers. More brilliant than all the others, then as now, was the anemone, or windflower. It grows along all the roads, and ranges in color from glowing crimson to brilliant purple. The plants reach a height of six inches. They spring to life every year after the first rains.

Jesus knew the hearts of men, and He put His finger on a major problem. Most people are worried about having enough money for food and clothing. Consider also the "elite," who take pride in having special foods and drinks to serve, or the latest fashions. Whether you are poor or rich, to dwell on these things displeases God.

God made us, just as He made the lilies of the field. But we are made in His image. How much more He must care for us!

Jesus does not discourage hard work or condemn wise planning. He opposes that obsession with temporal things which crowds out love—love for family, fellowman and God.

A boy barefoot on a freezing cold day was asked by a skeptical friend, "If God loves you, why doesn't He send you a pair of shoes?" The lad replied, "He told someone about me—but they forgot!" God knows our needs and will supply them in *His* time. We are not to worry about the future. God can provide all our needs day by day, just as He did in the desert for the Children of Israel.

God asks only one thing in exchange for His care. That is that we love Him and put Him first. What a small price to pay for the spiritual riches we have in Christ Jesus!

ASK YOURSELF: Whom do I think of most, others or myself? Are my days spent in worry or in faith? How important are any of my earthly cares, compared to the love of Christ?

PRAY ALONE TO GOD.

PRAY ALOUD: Father, as I consider the lilies, I remember Your love for me. I will trust You for my needs. I wish to live each day, one at a time, for You alone.

Field

PICK AN OBJECT: A large bush

PICK A LESSON: *His Way or My Way?*

GOD SAYS (Jonah 4: 5-7): "So Jonah went out of the city, and sat on the east side of the city, and there made him a booth, and sat under it in the shadow, till he might see what would become of the city. And the Lord God prepared a gourd, and made it to come up over Jonah, that it might be a shadow over his head, to deliver him from his grief. So Jonah was exceeding glad of the gourd. But God prepared a worm when the morning rose the next day, and it smote the gourd that it withered."

THINK ABOUT THIS: The lean-to that Jonah sat under that day was probably made of branches from large-leaf trees. But it was not enough to protect Jonah from the heat. So the Lord prepared a special plant. The Hebrew word for it means "nauseous to the taste"—what else but the castor oil tree! The plant is a very large bush, ten feet high, with broad, handsome leaves of rich green or sometimes bronze. The leaves have been likened to the hand of Christ, open and extended in blessing. From the tree an oil was extracted that was used as fuel for lamps. With even slight handling, it can wilt and wither, as did Jonah's that day.

God used this leafy plant as an object lesson for Jonah. It grew up, miraculously, overnight! It gave comfort and pleasure to Jonah in the intense heat of the day. But the next morning, it was destroyed by a worm. Now the sun beat down upon his head and a scorching wind blew on him until he almost wanted to die.

Jonah had been sulking because God chose to save the people of Nineveh when they repented of their sins. Jonah wanted them destroyed because of their evil deeds. But God said that, just as Jonah loved the plant, He loved the people of Nineveh. God didn't want a city of thousands to perish, any more than Jonah wanted the plant to die. Jonah loved his plant more than the people of Nineveh! God loved the people of Nineveh because He created them, and He took care of them. How much more important people are than plants!

ASK YOURSELF: Do I pout when God does things His way and not my way? If a sinner repented of his sin, would I feel bad that he did not get his "just reward" of punishment? Or would I rejoice with the angels for another soul added to the Kingdom? Could I ever love the things of nature more than people?

PRAY ALONE TO GOD.

PRAY ALOUD: Dear God, I want to tell the Good News of your salvation to everyone. Help me to obey Your will without comment or criticism. Forgive me for acting like Jonah sometimes. Let me love people more.

Wind

PICK A SPOT: Where the wind blows in different directions

PICK A LESSON: *Let's Grow Up*

GOD SAYS (Ephesians 4: 14, 15): "That we henceforth be no more children, tossed to and fro, and carried about with every wind of doctrine, by the sleight of men, and cunning craftiness, whereby they lie in wait to deceive; But speaking the truth in love, may grow up into him in all things, which is the head, even Christ."

THINK ABOUT THIS: When you play tennis outdoors and the wind changes direction, it means you have to change the way you play. A ball that was in bounds may be carried out of bounds, and vice-versa.

When you go sailing on the lake and the winds change, it makes a difference in how you steer the rudder. You must corral the craft into the wind, or else be tossed into the chilly blue waters.

Sometimes the wind comes up suddenly, from nowhere. It takes an expert water skier to stay up in the strong wind and waves. Or, if you're shooting arrows at the archery range, a deceiving gust of wind may blow your arrows off target, especially when shooting from some distance.

Wind can be very tricky—it can be strong, it can be soft; it can help cool you on a summer day and it can freeze you on a wintry day. Only the very practiced sportsperson can correct the swinging of a racket or steering of the sails in time. Only a very strong person can resist the wind's effect upon his skiing stance or the aim of his bow.

The Bible urges us to be strong and mature in our faith. We are not to be like children, who yield quickly to every impulse or pressure. We are to reject the false teachings of people who don't know God. Winds are unpredictable, deceitful! So are people who would convince you against the truth.

Satan uses sinners and weak Christians alike to lead young Christians astray. Newborn believers are like infants in the faith. They need nourishing spiritual food. Self-righteous "do-gooders" and pious legalists pick at the clothes, the hair, the habits of a babe in Christ. They are confusing the truth! A warning to Christians who really want to help is: Don't feed young people the popcorn and peanuts of Christian culture, when they need the milk and meat of the Word!

The truths of God are peaceful and pure. If you would share them with others, do it in love, or don't do it at all.

ASK YOURSELF: Do the winds of varying opinions sway my mind about Christ? Am I mature enough to evaluate and adjust my thinking for the greatest good for all concerned? Can I stand against the attacks of criticism? Have I ever been guilty of confusing God's newborn children? Has my attitude in sharing Christ been one of love?

PRAY ALONE TO GOD.

PRAY ALOUD: When I am tossed about by the winds of doubt: comfort, calm, and correct my vision. Let me see You only! Keep me witnessing, not out of duty but out of love! Keep me from harming those I seek to help. Help me grow in the knowledge and wisdom that comes from above.

Wind

PICK A SPOT: Where the wind blows (sailing)

PICK A LESSON: *Power, Panic, Peace*

GOD SAYS (Jonah 1: 4-10): "But as the ship was sailing along, suddenly the Lord flung a terrific wind over the sea, causing a great storm that threatened to send them to the bottom. Fearing for their lives, the desperate sailors shouted to their gods for help and threw the cargo overboard to lighten the ship. And all this time Jonah was sound asleep down in the hold. So the captain went down after him. 'What do you mean,' he roared, 'sleeping at a time like this? Get up and cry to your god, and see if he will have mercy on us and save us!' Then the crew decided to draw straws to see which of them had offended the gods and caused this terrible storm; and Jonah drew the short one. 'What have you done,' they asked, 'to bring this awful storm upon us?' . . . And he said, 'I am a Jew; I worship Jehovah, the God of heaven, who made the earth and sea.' Then he told them he was running away from the Lord" (*LB*).

THINK ABOUT THIS: If you go sailing, you know that the sails must obey the wind. The mainsail and the jib are controlled by ropes or rigging which catch the wind to give speed. With no wind, the craft would not move. The rudder gives direction. When you decide to turn around, you must do a "come about" by shifting the rudder quickly to the other side of the boat, being careful not to let the boom hit you. On a rough windy day, it may take two or more people sitting on the side toward the wind to keep the craft upright, but oh how it does sail! Waves roll over the bow and forcefully splash over you. It's exciting! But if you don't like sailing, you won't like it when it's rough.

And it must have been terribly rough for these sailors in Jonah's day, since the craft was large and it was about to sink because of the mighty wind. The sailors were not Christians. In a New Testament story (Matthew 8: 23-27) the sailors were disciples. But, like Jonah, Jesus was asleep in the boat. And in both cases the cry from the sailors was the same, "Wake up and save us before we perish." Panic comes to the heart of anyone who faces death. The difference comes in the way a Christian meets it.

How like Jonah we are today. We try so hard to run away from God, to do everything but what He wants us to. Jonah knew what to do, but he didn't do it. Wind was used by God to stop His servant from going too far. Perhaps God will use an object of His creation to get your attention if you're not following Him.

Wind is one of God's treasures (Psalm 135: 7). We must respect its power for good or bad. Much more, we must respect the Creator of the mighty wind, God our Savior.

ASK YOURSELF: When the wind blows fiercely through the trees, do I trust Him? When the wind blows gently and all is well, do I trust Him? How far have I strayed from the path of His perfect will for my life? What might it take for God to bring me back to Himself?

PRAY ALOUD: Thank You for the wind that blew Jonah back on the right course. Keep me trusting You completely when the winds of trouble stir up my soul. Give me boldness to speak of my love for You. Help me to obey Your will.

Wind

PICK A SPOT: When the wind blows weeds back and forth

PICK A LESSON: *Bouncing Back*

GOD SAYS (Matthew 11:2-7): "John the Baptist, who was now in prison, heard about all the miracles the Messiah was doing, so he sent his disciples to ask Jesus, 'Are you really the one we are waiting for, or shall we keep on looking?' Jesus told them, 'Go back to John and tell him about the miracles you've seen me do—the blind people I've healed, and the lame people now walking without help, and the cured lepers, and the deaf who hear, and the dead raised to life; and tell him about my preaching the Good News to the poor. Then give him this message, "Blessed are those who don't doubt me."' When John's disciples had gone, Jesus began talking about him to the crowds. 'When you went out into the barren wilderness to see John, what did you expect him to be like? Grass blowing in the wind?'" (*LB*).

THINK ABOUT THIS: We often see grass blowing in the wind. Sometimes it ripples like a wave on the seashore. The blades of grass are so supple that they bend easily and almost lie down. Then the wind stops and they stand up straight again.

The reed of Egypt is much like the grass we see each day. However, it is much taller. It is 12 inches high, yet so slender and yielding that it will lie perfectly flat under a gust of wind, and immediately spring back after the wind dies down.

John the Baptist is described as "a reed shaken with the wind" (verse 7). At this time in his life, he was discouraged and in prison. Being an outdoor man, he must have hated his confinement in prison. He may have been in ill health. He felt that his life was ending in its very prime, after only two years of labor for His Lord. And Jesus apparently was neglecting him by ministering over 100 miles away.

It's easy to doubt when you're downhearted! John sent his friends to Jesus, to ask Him if He really was the Christ. Deep in his heart, he knew the truth. But he needed reassurance. Jesus' response was not critical, but concise. *Go* and *tell* what you see and hear! Then he enumerated six things: the blind see, the lame walk, the lepers are clean, the deaf hear, the dead are raised, and the poor hear the Good News of eternal riches in Heaven. Then he added a Beatitude to take back to John: "Blessed are those who don't doubt!"

Do you doubt Him? How much trouble does it take you to doubt?

Like a reed after the wind has stopped, John's faith bounced back.

ASK YOURSELF: Am I so bent that I'm lying down, doubting God? Do I keep strong and fit spiritually so that when winds of trouble die down I can spring up again to full stature? Am I seeing changes in my life and in the lives of others because of the work of the Holy Spirit?

PRAY ALONE TO GOD.

PRAY ALOUD: Dear God, banish doubts from my mind. May I bolster believers by the testimony of miracles wrought in my life. Keep me upright when the winds of worry and trouble surround me.

Wind

PICK A SPOT: Grassy, where wind is blowing

PICK A LESSON: *The Holy Spirit*

GOD SAYS (John 3: 8): "The wind bloweth where it listeth, and thou hearest the sound thereof, but canst not tell whence it cometh, and whither it goeth: so is every one that is born of the Spirit."

THINK ABOUT THIS: As the wind howls around your tent at night, you listen to its voice. You know that if you stepped out, you wouldn't see it at all. Just before a summer rainstorm, you can hear the wind whistling through the trees, and see animals scurrying to their shelters.

John here compares the wind and the Holy Spirit. First, both are supreme or sovereign in their activities. Second, both are mysterious in their operations.

Wind is unpredictable; it is beyond man's control. The best weather experts can't even give the camp directors the perfect weather forecast. The wind can't be regulated by man's devices. So it is with the Spirit.

Wind is irresistible; it sweeps everything before it as in a tornado. So is the Spirit, when He comes in the fulness of His power. He breaks down man's prejudices, subdues his rebellious will, overcomes all opposition.

Wind is irregular. It moves softly, or may blow loudly and even roar. So is the Spirit. The new birth comes to some gently, to others with great emotion.

Wind is invisible. The Spirit also is invisible.

Wind is inscrutable. Its origin, nature, activities are beyond man's understanding. Activities of the Spirit, too, are secret; His workings mysterious.

Wind is indispensable. If calm were to continue indefinitely, all vegetation would die. So it is with the Spirit. Without Him there could be no spiritual life at all.

Wind is invigorating. Physicians order people to rest at mountain or seaside; wind restores health. So it is with the Spirit. He is the One who strengthens us from within, and energizes and empowers us to do God's will.

To summarize, the wind blows and we can hear it. These are two things we know. Where it goes, we don't know—it is a mystery. The Spirit gives new birth and person knows; these are facts. But how the Holy Spirit operates upon the soul to bring us to God, and reveal the deep things of Him, we don't know—it's a mystery. But, "Marvel not that I said unto thee, Ye must be born again" (John 3: 7). As the Spirit moves in our souls—as the wind moves the leaves—God fills our lives with peace and everlasting joy.

ASK YOURSELF: Does the Holy Spirit dwell within me? Have I been born of the Spirit? As I live the Christian life, does God's Spirit energize and empower me to do God's will?

PRAY ALONE TO GOD.

PRAY ALOUD: Thank You for the wind that blows to make things grow and to dry the earth. As the wind blows around us each day in the out-of-doors, we are reminded of the Holy Spirit who dwells within us. May He fill us and give us power over the evil forces that would destroy our souls. Come, Holy Spirit!

Wind

PICK A SPOT: By a lake

PICK A LESSON: *Listen and Obey*

GOD SAYS (Matthew 8: 23-27): "Then he got into a boat and started across the lake with his disciples. Suddenly a terrible storm came up, with waves higher than the boat. But Jesus was asleep. The disciples went to him and wakened him, shouting. 'Lord, save us! We're sinking!' But Jesus answered, 'O you men of little faith! Why are you so frightened?' Then he stood up and rebuked the wind and waves, and the storm subsided and all was calm. The disciples just sat there, awed! 'Who is this,' they asked themselves, 'that even the winds and the sea obey him?' " (*LB*).

THINK ABOUT THIS: This passage could read, "Then he got into a boat and started across the lake with his friends." It could be talking about you. Did you ride in a boat yesterday, or will you go today? Your selection of craft is greater than in Jesus' day. Their boats were all hand-powered. Yet we still love to take out the "good ol' " rowboat or swift canoe. Since many of the disciples were avid fishermen, they were used to handling boats. They were expert oarsmen.

This tells us that this was no ordinary storm. Being on the lake a lot, these men had been caught in all kinds of weather and were experienced in bringing a craft to shore. But this time it was different. A good sailor will watch the darkening clouds and rising winds and not venture out. This storm came up *suddenly*. We say a person is "caught" in a storm, meaning it came up without warning. Ever been caught in a storm?

Jesus had talked to large crowds all day, and He was tired. So He fell asleep. Fear of the water usually prevents most of us from going to sleep in a boat. But Jesus created the water, and He had no fear! He was probably exhausted, just as we might have been! The ship was being covered with waves and was rocking fiercely; still He slept. Excitedly the worried disciples shook Him and shouted, "Save us, or we perish!"

What a contrast! The believer in panic, and Jesus in peace! God knows our frailties so well. We must believe in Him to help us. We must believe in Him to save us from our sins or we will perish (John 3: 16). For the Christian, faith in God is essential when the winds of adversity come.

Awakening, Jesus first rebuked the disciples for their lack of faith. Perhaps He was saying, "Since you have the power of God within you by faith, you could have prayed." Or, "Why are you so afraid? You know I am with you and will always protect my children." Then Jesus rebuked, literally "muzzled," the wind and waves. Immediately there was a great calm! Again, a vivid contrast. Suddenly—a storm; immediately—a calm! Only the Creator of heavens and earth could do this!

His *creation* always obeys Him, but not His creatures (John 1: 11.) When someone in authority rebukes you, how do you respond? The animals of the forest, the fish, the wind and the waves—all obey Him. Since each one of us is a special creation of God, made in His image, how much more should we obey Him.

ASK YOURSELF: How great is my God that even the winds and waves obey Him? The Lord is ready to save me; am I ready to receive His salvation and His help in time of need? How much faith do I have to rebuke the winds of adversity from Satan's hand?

PRAY ALONE TO GOD.

PRAY ALOUD: Calm my fears on the sea of life, as You calmed the winds of the sea. Give me faith to conquer the problems that I face. Thank You for saving me from sin and death. Let me live in obedience to Your every command.

Fire

PICK AN OBJECT: A fire

PICK A LESSON: *Starting a Fire*

GOD SAYS (Proverbs 26:20, 21): "Fire goes out for lack of fuel, and tensions disappear when gossip stops. A quarrelsome man starts fights as easily as a match sets fire to paper" (*LB*).

THINK ABOUT THIS: The veteran camper knows how to make a good fire lay. He knows that first the ground must be cleared. Then tinder (pencil-thin sticks), kindling (wrist-thickness wood), and fuel (large logs) must be collected in piles and if necessary weather-protected by tarp. Next the fire is built within a circle or "V" shape. Several small sticks are propped up together in a "teepee" shape. Dried leaves or grasses make good tinder, too.

Leaving some air between the tinder materials, put on the kindling, carefully building up the "teepee." Firewood is last; it can be built around the teepee in log cabin fashion, or in a variety of other ways. Finally the fire is lit, from the leeward side (away from the wind). And if you've done a good job, you'll have a great fire in no time.

The Scripture tells us that if we fail to put the large logs on, the fire will go out—which is very true. Tinder only burns for seconds, kindling for minutes, but fuel logs for hours.

The lesson we learn is that when a person starts a story, and people pass it around, and keep adding to it, it gets very hot and vicious. But when there is no fuel, the gossip will die down and even stop. Gossip can hurt people much more than a physical beating. A person who passes gossip, or adds fuel to the fire, is only trying to elevate himself. And in the end he feels worse, not better, for having done it. Perhaps it gets so hot that a person is intensely persecuted, even though innocent. Then how does a gossip feel?

God honors those who are able to tame their tongues. James says that the tongue is a small thing which can do enormous damage. A great forest can be set on fire by one tiny spark. And the tongue is a flame of fire, James tells us. It is full of wickedness, and poisons every part of the body. The tongue is set on fire by hell itself, and can turn our lives into a blazing flame of destruction and disaster (James 3: 5, 6).

A second lesson pointed out in the passage is that a person who starts fights with others (verbal or physical) does it as easily as a match sets fire to paper. Paper is the fastest tinder that you can use to start a fire. Newspaper, wadded up tightly into a ball, is commonly used by campers. A quarrelsome person is said to have a "short fuse," meaning that he spouts off at the slightest provocation. The Bible says that the wounds this person inflicts go deep (Proverbs 26: 22).

ASK YOURSELF: Am I a gossip? How well do I control my tongue? When was the last time I said something that hurt someone else? How quick am I to start arguments and fights with others?

PRAY ALONE TO GOD.

PRAY ALOUD: Dear God, help me guard my tongue from saying evil things. Let me stop gossip whenever I can. Give me grace to be quiet when others provoke me. Forgive me for hurting others and hurting You. Keep my tongue from speaking evil today.

Fire

PICK A SPOT: Beside a very hot fire

PICK A LESSON: *Young Men in a Hot Spot*

GOD SAYS (Daniel 3: 25-27): " 'Well, look!' Nebuchadnezzar shouted. 'I see *four* men, unbound, walking around in the fire, and they aren't even hurt by the flames! And the fourth looks like a god!' Then Nebuchadnezzar came as close as he could to the open door of the flaming furnace and yelled: 'Shadrach, Meshach, and Abednego, servants of the Most High God! Come out! Come here!' So they stepped out of the fire. . . . not a hair of their heads was singed; their coats were unscorched, and they didn't even smell of smoke" (*LB*).

THINK ABOUT THIS: In a day when capital punishment is questioned, it may seem grossly cruel to burn in a furnace those who have merely disobeyed a law. Why was Nebuchadnezzar so cruel?

You talk about hot! How hot a fire have you ever witnessed? Picture a reflector-type fire 100 times bigger than you would ever build. Put the fire at the base of a steep cliff; put a wall on each side, and a barrier in the front for a door. As you see this gigantic inferno in your mind, picture three young Jewish officers standing above it on the cliff, clothed and bound. Suddenly the flames leap as high as the top of the cliff, and soldiers standing near the Jews are burned to death. The three men fall down into the midst of the fire. Yet in a moment they are standing, unbound and walking in the flames. They step out of the furnace at the king's command, completely unscathed. A miracle, yes! And only because God was with them.

Three promises stand out. There is the *promise of persecution*. Christians should expect the furnace of persecution, if they live lives dedicated to Christ. It's easy to give in and go along with the crowd. These men trusted God to glorify Himself either in their lives or by their deaths. We should expect persecution, since God promised it (Philippians 1: 29; John 15: 18-20).

The *promise of preservation* tells us God will never forsake His own when they go through a fiery trial. He may not keep us out of the hot spots, but He will go with us and bring us through for His glory. When the king looked into the furnace, he saw four men—one of them was Jesus Christ! Jesus walked with them; He untied them and kept them from being harmed. They didn't even smell of the fire. Smell your own clothes! If you've even been around a campfire, you'll smell like it!

The third promise is the *promise of promotion*. These men were actually better off for having gone through the fire! It is worth danger and trial to know how near the Lord can be to us. The fire set them free from their bonds, just as suffering for Christ today gives us joyful liberty and freedom from sin. Their experience glorified God before others (I Corinthians 6: 19, 20) and the king promoted them and gave them honors.

ASK YOURSELF: How true am I to my Lord? Am I strong enough to go through the fiery trials of life? How often have I chosen the way of righteousness regardless of what friends have said?

PRAY ALONE TO GOD.

PRAY ALOUD: Dear God, keep me close to You. Strengthen my faith. Help me stand against the trials and temptations of life. Let me be willing to suffer, in order to be rewarded together with You.

Fire

PICK A SPOT: By a fire

PICK A LESSON: *God's Refinery*

GOD SAYS (Malachi 3: 2, 3): But who can live when He appears? Who will be able to endure His coming? For He will be like a blazing fire refining precious metal. And He will be like strong soap, able to bleach the dirtiest garments. Like a refiner of silver he will sit and closely watch as the dross is burned away. (Paraphrased.)

THINK ABOUT THIS: Fire is a good example of something that in itself is neither all good nor all bad. This is true today, as it always was. Fire can be used to light the trail by the flame of a Coleman lantern, or as God did, by a "pillar of fire" each night for the Israelites (Exodus 13: 21, 22). It can be used to boil food or charcoal-broil a steak. Jesus and His disciples cooked fish over the open fire one morning on the beach (John 21).

On a cool evening, campfire warms the body and soul. The apostle Paul and his shipmates gathered around a bonfire to dry themselves out on the island of Malta (Acts 28: 1).

Fire can burn away impurities in all kinds of metals, and then helps form them into usable items. Fire is used to melt glass, which can then be twisted into beautiful shapes.

On the other hand, fire can burn up a steak. It can burn you if you get too close. It burns big buildings, homes, even a tent. It burns down mighty forests with the touch of a match, destroying all the living things in its way.

In our Bible, fire is used for the ultimate good of its object. A blazing fire refines silver. The ore is put into a small furnace, where the lead impurities are oxidized until the silver bath is clear. The metal is cast in molds to make silver bars.

Jesus Christ is seeking to cleanse and purify the people of God, as Malachi prophesied. He does this through the trials we face in life. They test our faith.

Fire is a friend to those whose names are written in the Book of Life. But an eternal Lake of Fire awaits those who come unprepared to God's last judgment.

ASK YOURSELF: Is Christ lighting the path I walk today? (Read Psalm 119: 105.) Are "fiery" trials preparing me *now* for the great joy of His second coming? (Read I Peter 1: 6, 7.)

PRAY ALONE TO GOD.

PRAY ALOUD: Dear God, I will follow the narrow path as You light the way. Help me to yield to Your cleansing power. Purify me now in obedience to Your Word.

Fire

PICK A TIME: By the morning fire

PICK A LESSON: *Judgment by Fire*

GOD SAYS (Genesis 19: 23-25): "The sun was rising as Lot reached the village. Then the Lord rained down fire and flaming tar from heaven upon Sodom and Gomorrah, and utterly destroyed them, along with the other cities and villages of the plain, eliminating all life—people, plants, and animals" (*LB*).

THINK ABOUT THIS: The sun may be rising where you sit at your campsite. What kind of a day will it be? Will it be a glorious day, filled with the goodness of God's blessings? Or might it be a day of judgment for you?

Lot, backslidden nephew of Abraham, was in the sinful city of Sodom when two men came in the evening. Lot welcomed them and invited them to come to his home. They said they would sleep in the streets, but he insisted they come home with him. He made a large meal for them. When it was time to retire, the men of the city surrounded the house. The two strangers—who were in reality angels—blinded the men outside so that they couldn't find the door. The angels said, "Get your family and get out of the city quickly; the Lord is going to destroy it." Lot rushed to tell all his family, but few believed him.

Near dawn, the angels grabbed his hand and the hands of his wife and two daughters and rushed them to safety. At Lot's insistence the angels let them flee to the small village of Zoar rather than go to the mountains. And then it happened. Fire and flaming tar came down and burned up everyone and everything.

Abraham rose early that morning and hurried to the place where he had pleaded with the Lord to save Lot. He saw columns of smoke and fumes, as from a furnace, rising from the cities there.

For the lack of ten righteous people in the whole city (Lot's family plus any two neighbors), God destroyed all in sight. What an unconvincing witness Lot must have been!

Dr. Warren Wiersbe says that this is a picture of the wrath to come. When men think there is peace and safety, then destruction will fall upon them (I Thessalonians 5). The Lord rescued Lot for Abraham's sake; and He will deliver His Church from the wrath to come for Jesus' sake (I Thessalonians 1: 8; 5: 9). The cities of Sodom and Gomorrah, full of lust of every kind, destroyed by fire, continue to be a warning to us that there is a hell in which sinners are punished (Jude 7).

The angels snatched Lot's hands and guided him to safety before it was too late. How many people around you are destined for judgment? Will you snatch them from the fire before it's too late? Jude 22, 23 says, "Try to help those who argue against you. Be merciful to those who doubt. Save some by snatching them as from the very flames of hell itself" (*LB*).

ASK YOURSELF: Is my name written in the Book of Life? Am I as poor a witness as Lot was? Who have I snatched from the flames?

PRAY ALONE TO GOD.

PRAY ALOUD: I thank You that You who are the Judge of all men are a Father to me. I will learn from Your small daily judgments of my deeds, in the confidence that You will save me in the Last Day.

Fire

PICK A SPOT: Beside a fire

PICK A LESSON: *Astrologers and Stargazers*

GOD SAYS (Isaiah 47: 13, 14): "You have advisors by the ton—your astrologers and stargazers, who try to tell you what the future holds. But they are as useless as dried grass burning in the fire. They cannot even deliver themselves! You'll get no help from them at all. Theirs is no fire to sit beside to make you warm!" (*LB*).

THINK ABOUT THIS: One of the best things about a fire is getting warmth from it. You spread your fingers in the heat as it rises from the blazing fire or hot coals. The heat seems to go right through you, warming you inside and out.

The Bible likens the warmth of a fire to the advice you get from people. By inference, good advice offers warmth to the soul, but bad advice offers only a glimmer of light, then disappears. Good advice is like warming yourself continually by the fire; bad advice is the flash of light you get by throwing dried grass on a fire. Try it! You'll see! It's gone before you can count to ten.

Dried grass or weeds is at best a "fast tinder." Tinder is used only to get a fire started. It ignites quickly, then disappears as larger wood fibers begin to burn.

The advice you get from the multitude of astrologers and stargazers today is but a flash of bright light, appearing for a very short time. In a day when you may often be asked, "What's your sign (of the Zodiac)?" astrology is, of course, a common concern. People count on finding out ahead of time what the day will hold for those with their particular birthdates. They get their advice in the morning paper, see it on TV, or consult their personal horoscopes. Weddings, parties, even funerals are scheduled by the stars.

The Bible says that this is foolish. You will get no real help at all from astrologers. They can't predict the future. Nor can they cause fortune to smile upon themselves. Good things happen only according to God's plan.

If you're looking for good advice to make you feel warm and happy and comfortable inside or out, sit by the fire of God's Word.

There's really only One who can foretell your future. He is the One who holds the future in His hands, the Lord Jesus Christ.

ASK YOURSELF: Upon whom do I depend for guidance about my future? Do I lean on friends or "experts" for advice about my life? Or do I go to men of God and the Word for insight concerning His will for my life?

PRAY ALONE TO GOD.

PRAY ALOUD: Teach me more from Your Word about what the future holds for my life. Let me lean upon You to guide me through the mysteries that lie before me. I seek to center my hope on things above, where nothing can corrupt or steal from my inheritance. Let me warm myself by the fire of Your love.

Weather

PICK A TIME: During or after rain

PICK A LESSON: *Refreshing Rain*

GOD SAYS (Psalms 72: 6; 104: 13): "May the reign of this son of mine be as gentle and fruitful as the springtime rains upon the grass—like showers that water the earth! . . . He sends rain upon the mountains and fills the earth with fruit" (*LB*).

THINK ABOUT THIS: Listen to the gentle pitter-patter of raindrops on the thirsty leaves, on the canvas tent top, or on the parched brown dirt around the campfire. Doesn't it feel special? The rain is sort of chilly, sweet smelling, refreshing. God has just decided to water His earth—to give it a shower because He knows it needs it. He's giving His plants a long, cool drink, His trees a dusting off, and His creatures big and small a good bath.

These verses contain two words that rhyme: reign and rain. Reigning King David looks past his own sons to the Messianic Son, Jesus Christ. The gentle springtime rains whose droplets contain just the right chemicals to bring growth to all His creation are likened to Christ's reign over the earth. He came to the just and the unjust. He was warm and gentle. Like the touch of rain, whatever He touched was filled with new life.

Just as we scurry for cover when caught in the rain on the hillside, trail, or canoeing the lake streams, God would like to swoop us up into His loving arms and say, "Come inside, here to abide with Me." The rain itself is a shower of blessing, too wonderful to comprehend.

Let the rain remind us that God is good, He's telling us that we, too, need refreshing. Our refreshment comes from stopping often to talk with Him. Tell Him of your problems. Then be still and let Him talk to you. It will be a spiritual shower from God to make you feel refreshed and like new.

Like plants, we will be enabled to bear fruit for Him.

ASK YOURSELF: When was the last time I took a good spiritual shower? How truly clean and fresh do I want to be—inside? Do I give a sweet savor to others? Do my words bring showers of blessing to others?

PRAY ALONE TO GOD.

PRAY ALOUD: Dear Lord, Thank You for the soft refreshing rain that You send. Thank You, Jesus, who loved me enough to die for me. Cleanse me now by Your Spirit. Make me active in showering your love to those around me.

Weather

PICK A TIME: Just before a rain

PICK A LESSON: *Elijah and the Rainstorm*

GOD SAYS (I Kings 18: 41-45): "Elijah said to Ahab, 'Go and enjoy a good meal! For I hear a mighty rainstorm coming!' . . . Elijah climbed to the top of Mount Carmel [and prayed. He sent his servant to look out to sea for a cloud, but he couldn't see anything, until the seventh time] . . . his servant told him, 'I saw a little cloud about the size of a man's hand rising from the sea.' Then Elijah shouted, 'Hurry to Ahab and tell him to get into his chariot and get down the mountain, or he'll be stopped by the rain!' And sure enough, the sky was soon black with clouds, and a heavy wind brought a terrific rainstorm. Ahab left hastily for Jezreel, and the Lord gave special strength to Elijah so that he was able to run ahead of Ahab's chariot to the entrance of the city!" (*LB*).

THINK ABOUT THIS: The sun rises high and bright in the morning and you think it's going to be a really nice day. Then about mid-morning, clouds gather—first one, then many, with a silver lining. Soon they bump together and begin to shut out the sun's rays. It's *then* that we look up to see the sky (only when the light is *shut off*). We see the mass of clouds turning gray. Soon the whole sky is dark, and the winds blow fiercely, bringing rain.

At camp you begin to take in all the things that might get wet. You quickly cover the wood supply with tarp. You pull down the tent flaps. If you're on the trail, you start running back as fast as you can, especially if you have forgotten a raincoat! If you're at the beach, you must run to shelter for protection from lightning. Even under a tree is not safe!

Elijah prayed for rain. He kept sending his servant to see if he could see the signs of rain. Six times he returned with a "no" answer. The seventh time he saw a tiny white cloud, then more clouds, then a blackened sky, heavy winds, and finally a terrific rainstorm.

When God sends judgments on us, he always gives us warning signals. He warns us by bringing trials into our lives to bring us back to Himself. If we continue to turn away, to shut off all the light from Heaven, He will let the black clouds roll together, and bring judgment upon our lives. We must be sensitive to His Holy Spirit and let God teach us His way before it is too late.

This story ends on a humorous note. Sometimes when we ask God for things, He brings them more quickly than we had expected! Can you visualize Elijah seeing the storm coming and having no means of transportation? He knew he would have to run 15 miles, all the way back to town. What a race that must have been! I surely would have liked to see Elijah, God's prophet, running a foot race with Ahab's chariot and horses. The Bible tells us that God gave him extra strength to do it. Even when we ask for more than we can ordinarily handle, He gives us extra strength to perform the task when the pressure is on!

ASK YOURSELF: How persistent am I in prayer for seeing God's will done? Am I sensitive to the Holy Spirit to perceive what God is trying to teach me through the trials of life? Is God able to perform abundantly those things for which I ask Him?

PRAY ALONE TO GOD.

PRAY ALOUD: Thank You for Elijah's example of faith and trust in You. Help me to see the signs of Your blessings as well as your judgments in my life. Keep me trusting always and depending on You for extra strength in time of need.

Weather

PICK A TIME: When a rainbow appears

PICK A LESSON: *God's Promise*

GOD SAYS (Genesis 9: 12-17): "And I seal this promise with this sign: I have placed my rainbow in the clouds as a sign of my promise until the end of time, to you and to all the earth. When I send clouds over the earth, the rainbow will be seen in the clouds, and I will remember my promise to you and to every being, that never again will the floods come and destroy all life. For I will see the rainbow in the cloud and remember my eternal promise to every living being" (*LB*).

THINK ABOUT THIS: To see a rainbow in the sky during a soft summer rain is always an exciting thing. On some days the bow is sharp and beautiful. All seven colors of the spectrum are present in every rainbow. Scientists say that a rainbow always appears in the sky opposite the sun. It's almost as if God were looking at it too, to remember His promise. The person looking at the rainbow has his back to the sun. The rainbow is due to the bending and reflection of the sun's rays when they are shining on raindrops in the sky.

The white light of the sun is composed of all colors mixed together; but when this white light passes through an area of rain, the rays composing it are bent to different degrees and so are forced apart. When they reach the back of the rain, these separated rays—violet, indigo, blue, green, yellow, orange, red—are reflected back to the eye. You sometimes see the same colors when sun shines on the spray kicked up by a speed boat.

No one can ever see the other side of the rainbow. He would be looking right into the sun. The higher the sun is in the sky, the smaller the arc of the rainbow. At noon in summer, we can't see a rainbow because the sun is never at our backs, but overhead. A person on top of a mountain may sometimes see almost a complete circle, not just an arc.

God grew weary of the sins of man. He even "regretted" that He had made man on the earth (Genesis 6: 6). So He decided to destroy the world with a global flood. It rained many days and nights, and every living thing not in the ark was destroyed (Genesis 7: 4). Now, every time the rainbow appears, it's a reminder of His destruction of mankind. And it's a promise to us that the world will never again be destroyed by water.

As we think of Christ's great love in coming to earth to die for our sins, and as we think of His promise in the sky each time it rains, we must also think of His justice in judging the world for its sin. The world is not getting any better. Moral and ethical values are degraded daily.

Each one of us should be aware that our days are numbered, and so are the days of all mankind. Next time we see a rainbow in the sky, let us praise Him for His promise. Let us pray for His protection from the evil in the world lest we, too, be destroyed. God is longsuffering, but how we must grieve Him when we give in to sin. Let us go to our knees often and beg His help before evil ways overtake our lives and the way back to Him is long and hard. He is always ready to receive one who is truly sorry for his sin.

ASK YOURSELF: Have I grieved my Lord? Lying, cheating, stealing, gossiping are sins in God's sight; do I consider them so bad? How much am I like the sinners of Noah's day? What do I think of when I see a rainbow?

PRAY ALONE TO GOD.

PRAY ALOUD: Thank You for the rainbow in the sky when it rains. May You always rain down blessings upon me. Keep me from letting sin reign in my body. Forgive me for the times I have sinned against You.

Weather

PICK A TIME: During snow, or on a hot summer day

PICK A LESSON: *Faithfulness and Honor*

GOD SAYS (Proverbs 25:13; 26:1): "A faithful employee is as refreshing as [snow] in the hot summertime. . . . Honor doesn't go with fools any more than snow with summertime" (*LB*).

THINK ABOUT THIS: On a hot summer day, when the heat beats down and you can't escape the steamy, sticky feeling, the vision of a beautiful snowy day almost makes you feel better.

Sometimes the reverse is true. Perhaps you've been skiing, sledding, or snowmobiling and your fingers and toes sting from the frost. Oh, to feel the hot sun beating down upon your body on the beach!

The Bible uses this to describe how we feel when someone who says he will do something is true to his word. If you are a camp leader or a parent, you know what it means to have a child be unfaithful. After being disappointed time after time, you finally get to the point where you don't trust him.

When someone says he will do something, do you trust him? If not, you've probably been conditioned by the unfaithful.

Dr. Henry Brandt helped me when he said, "Don't *ex*pect, but *in*spect." Now when I ask people to do things, I always check up on them, by offering to help in any way I can. Do camp counselors always perform all their duties, or must they be checked on at times? Most often people *do* need to be reminded of their responsibilities. But how refreshing to find someone who "didn't forget."

In our second passage, God is teaching us another lesson in the snow and the summertime. On a hot summer day, you would never see snow. Nor would you feel the hot humidity of a summer day in the wintertime. And honor isn't found in fools. "The fool hath said in his heart, There is no God" (Psalm 14:1). The fool thinks only of himself. He doesn't hold himself accountable to God.

ASK YOURSELF: At the end of life's road, will He say to me, "Well done, thou good and faithful servant"? Does the snow remind me of my faithfulness to man and to God? Am I faithful to the tasks assigned to me? Sometimes? Always?

PRAY ALONE TO GOD.

PRAY ALOUD: Thank You for the snow that brightens our lives. Thank You for the seasons we can enjoy—the heat in summer, and the snow in winter. May I seek You first, and be faithful in serving You. I will try to bring the fool to the wisdom of God.

Weather

PICK A TIME: Snowy weather

PICK A LESSON: *Hidden Treasure*

GOD SAYS (Job 38: 1-4, 22): "Then the Lord answered Job from the whirlwind: 'Why are you using your ignorance to deny my providence? Now get ready to fight, for I am going to demand some answers from you, and you must reply. Where were you when I laid the foundations of the earth? Tell me, if you know so much.... Have you visited the treasuries of the snow, or seen where hail is made and stored?'" (*LB*).

THINK ABOUT THIS: When we begin to reflect on the treasures of the snow, we think first of the clouds above, where the intricate and beautiful snow crystals are formed. Upon the tops of high mountains, whether these be situated within the frigid, temperate, or tropical zones, snow falls each year. Above a certain height, called the snowline, snow remains permanently.

The feature of chief interest and importance concerning the internal structure of snow crystals is the occurrence of minute air tubes. Each flake is intricately formed by a Master Designer. Each is different from every other. Though tiny as a pinhead, each is perfectly symmetrical. How magnificent are the mysteries of God's creative power.

By asking Job these questions and many more, God was trying to help Job see that even the trials which he suffered were part of God's great design. Each of our lives, like a snowflake, is worked upon by God.

God asked questions that no one could answer, especially Job in his broken condition. God asked if the rain has a father (vs. 28). Where does dew come from?

Who is the mother of the ice and frost—for the water changes and turns to ice, as hard as a rock (vss. 29, 30).

Job had no right to question or criticize God. His responsibility was rather to accept gladly the truth that God is in charge of His creation.

ASK YOURSELF: How often do I question God's working in my life? When I see snow piled by our cabin, do I think of how many million different snowflakes are lying there? How great is God to me? Am I willing to trust Him for strength to undergo all the trials of life? Do I have the faith of Job, to suffer as he suffered and still to trust in God?

PRAY ALONE TO GOD.

PRAY ALOUD: Thank You, Lord, for the white snow that reminds me of Your love to me. For though my sins were as scarlet, You made me as white as snow.

Mountain

PINNACLES OF PRAISE (Pages 77-90)
Mountaintop experiences with Jesus in Matthew

PICK A SPOT: Go to a hill each day of the week. Perhaps a different one each day would be possible. Today a very high hill is appropriate. Have the group stand and view the surrounding countryside. What kind of feeling do you get?

PICK A LESSON: *Testings of Jesus*

GOD SAYS (Matthew 4: 8-10; read Matthew 4: 1-7 as background): "Next Satan took him to the peak of a very high mountain and showed him the nations of the world and all their glory. 'I'll give it all to you,' he said, 'if you will only kneel and worship me.' 'Get out of here, Satan,' Jesus told him. 'The Scriptures say, "Worship only the Lord God. Obey only him." ' Then Satan went away, and angels came and cared for Jesus" (*LB*).

THINK ABOUT THIS: Suppose you were in the woods for 40 days and hadn't eaten anything! How hungry would you be? What would you be willing to do to get food? Would you be hungry enough to turn a stone into bread, knowing you could do it, and at the prodding of a powerful man? Jesus was very hungry. But He refused to be the pawn of Satan. He said, "Man shall not live by bread alone, but by every word that proceedeth out of the mouth of God." In our day, former Vietnam POWs have told us that, starving, they clung to their faith in God and His promise to deliver them. Their faith was stronger than the temptation facing them because of their hunger.

Christ's answer to Satan's second test was also a[n] emphatic no: Don't you know that the Scripture say[s] not to put the Lord your God to such a foolish test?

The third and final temptation came at the top [of] a high hill or mountain. Satan had the power to projec[t] for Jesus a panoramic view of all the nations of th[e] world. Satan said, "I'll give it all to you, if you wi[ll] only kneel and worship me." Jesus Christ knew tha[t] He was Lord over all the kingdoms of the world. Bu[t] He also knew the things He must suffer as a ma[n] before He would sit down at the right hand of God i[n] the throne room of Heaven. He thought of the spittin[g,] the name calling, the harassment, the crown of thorn[s,] the heavy cross, the piercing of the nails in His hand[s] and feet, the spear in His side. But He also thought [of] His Father who would give Him strength to go throug[h] these trials. He was patient, knowing there could be n[o] shortcuts to the coming of His Kingdom.

ASK YOURSELF: Was Jesus really tempted, since He wa[s] God? (Yes.) James 1:13 says that God cannot b[e] tempted. But Hebrews 4:15 tells us Jesus was tempte[d] *as a man* in all the ways that we are. How did Jes[us] meet the temptation each time? By quoting Scriptur[e.] We can do the same thing—if we know God's Word.

PRAY ALONE TO GOD.

PRAY ALOUD: Help me to trust You fully for strengt[h] in time of temptation. May I look to Your Word co[n]tinually for guidance in my life. And may I neve[r] foolishly test You, but fully depend upon You fo[r] everything.

Mountain

PICK A SPOT: Near or on a hill or mountain

PICK A LESSON: *Teachings of Jesus, I*

GOD SAYS (Matthew 5: 1-4): "One day as the crowds were gathering, he went up the hillside with his disciples and sat down and taught them there. 'Humble men are very fortunate!' he told them, 'for the Kingdom of Heaven is given to them. Those who mourn are fortunate! for they shall be comforted'" (*LB*).

THINK ABOUT THIS: As you gaze at the hillside, whether it is near or far away, sense the presence of Jesus Christ with you.

Think of this setting. Jesus saw the crowds following Him, who came from many regions (Matthew 4: 25). They pressed close around Him, tugging at His clothes, wanting Him to teach them and heal them. But feeling a need to speak alone with His disciples, He went to a secluded hillside and sat down to rest. His disciples came and joined Him. To these believers Jesus addressed the "Sermon on the Mount." He gave His guidance to those who loved Him, so that they could share it with others when He was gone.

Jesus began by saying: you will be happiest when you are humble. (What did He mean by "humble"? Perhaps He meant that we should know ourselves, and recognize our faults as well as our assets.) Jesus knew that the disciples would be pressed by crowds when He was gone, and would be worshiped when they performed miracles. Perhaps they would be tempted to be puffed up, proud! So He reminded them not to think more highly of themselves than they ought to. As their reward He promised them the Kingdom of Heaven.

Jesus could also foresee that there would be many occasions when our hearts would be sad, when we would see men turn from the truth, when we would encounter evil or see a brother persecuted for Christ. So He said: happy are you that sorrow and grieve for others, for you shall be comforted. (Only when our hearts are warm and tender toward God can we feel real compassion and sorrow for those around us who are in deep trouble.)

ASK YOURSELF: Am I humble? Do I give God credit for my health, my wisdom, my abilities? Or do I love to heap praise to myself whenever I get a chance? How tender is my heart toward others—those going through hard times?

PRAY ALONE TO GOD.

PRAY ALOUD: God, I praise You for all that You enable me to do here on earth, and for all Your material and spiritual blessings. They are Your gifts, and no cause for personal pride. May I be more sympathetic to others' needs.

Mountain

PICK A SPOT: Near or on a hill or mountain

PICK A LESSON: *Teachings of Jesus, II*

GOD SAYS (Matthew 5: 5, 6): "The meek and lowly are fortunate! for the whole wide world belongs to them. Happy are those who long to be just and good, for they shall be completely satisfied" (*LB*).

"Blessed are the meek: for they shall inherit the earth. Blessed are they which do hunger and thirst after righteousness: for they shall be filled."

THINK ABOUT THIS: Jesus taught His disciples that happiness belongs to the meek. What does it mean to be meek? Is it the same as weak? (No.) When our varsity girls' volleyball team was playing another college, one of the quiet girls—but a good athlete—failed to spike a well-set ball, merely giving it a tap. The assistant coach, sitting beside me, said: "Oh-oh. Jeannie let her meekness turn to weakness!" Her meekness was a great asset; her weakness was not.

The world honors those who are meek, who are calm and confident, and not quick to fight back when provoked. Jesus says that, for those who can take it, the whole world belongs to them!

He also taught them on the hillside that day that those who long to do what's right will be happy. How many times have people chided you for trying to do what's right? If you're a grownup, perhaps you didn't take a coffee break at work because you were anxious to get the job done. Or maybe you worked at something extra long when others quit early, and you did it without pay. Do you let amused remarks from others deter you from doing what you know to be right? You shouldn't! But, just maybe, you were doing something in order to brag about it, to be proud. In that case what you did isn't good, is it? Only when you do what's right with a sincere heart and to please the Lord, can you be happy.

ASK YOURSELF: What will it take to make me a meek person? Can God make me into a meek person? If I want Him to, He can! In my desire to do what's right, have I been boastful or proud? What can I do about it?

PRAY ALONE TO GOD.

PRAY ALOUD: Dear God, give me true happiness by helping me to be slow to speak, and slow to anger. Give me a sincere heart in my desire to do what is right. Keep me from the sin of pride!

Mountain

PICK A SPOT: On a hill or mountain

PICK A LESSON: *Teachings of Jesus, III*

GOD SAYS (Matthew 5: 7, 8): "Happy are the kind and merciful, for they shall be shown mercy. Happy are those whose hearts are pure, for they shall see God" (*LB*).

THINK ABOUT THIS: Here we are again, sitting on the hillside at the feet of Jesus as He teaches His chosen ones.

We have learned that:
> God loves those who think of themselves correctly.
> God loves those who sorrow and grieve for others.
> God loves those who can patiently take criticism.
> God loves those who sincerely desire to do right.

Jesus' fifth teaching is that people who are kind to others will be happy. This is no secret. Remember the time you loaned your buddy your toothpaste, or when you did a camp chore for someone else? It made you feel good inside. When we start doing helpful things for others, we find that others want to do things for us. What we sow, we reap, whether it be good or bad! Proverbs says a man must show himself friendly to have friends (18: 24).

Mercy is a quality we think of often in a negative sense. We say, "He is merciless." We mean that this person is hard, cruel, relentless, unforgiving! When God tells us to be merciful it means kind, loving, forgiving—forgiving, anyone who makes fun of us, who says a cutting remark, who spreads a false rumor, who tries to put us down in any way. That's not easy! If we want to be forgiven, we must forgive others.

Purity is a quality of character rarely found. In a wicked world, God's children must stay close by Him for daily cleansing. The heart of a person refers in Scripture to the center of being or the core of life. A child of God must not only be clean on the outside, but clean through and through. When young people are out on dates, it's sometimes difficult to act pure. When worldly temptations come, it's hard to be pure. But God promises a reward for those who keep themselves pure. They will see Him face to face.

To be pure, in the strict sense, means to be unspotted by evil. Only God can give us a truly pure heart, and only when we are pure will we be brought into the presence of God.

ASK YOURSELF: Do I want to be really happy? Do I show kindness and forgiveness to others at all times? Is it possible to be pure through and through?

PRAY ALONE TO GOD.

PRAY ALOUD: God, grant me Your Spirit so that I will be kind to others and forgive them when they err in any way. Help me to be pure in thought, word, and deed.

Mountain

PICK A SPOT: On a hill or mountain

PICK A LESSON: *Teachings of Jesus, IV*

GOD SAYS (Matthew 5: 9, 10): "Happy are those who strive for peace—they shall be called the sons of God. Happy are those who are persecuted because they are good, for the Kingdom of Heaven is theirs" (*LB*).

THINK ABOUT THIS: These are the seventh and eighth lessons Jesus taught His disciples on the mountain that day. We often call these eight The Beatitudes. Notice that the word "attitudes" is contained in this word. That's exactly what Christ was teaching. It doesn't matter what a person has in the way of looks, clothes, talents. All that really matters is what kind of attitude he has toward others. You can have everything the world can afford, but if you don't have love, you are nothing (I Corinthians 13).

One way to find happiness is to strive for peace. Peace starts at home or at camp. Think over the last few days! Have you refused to do your part in cleaning up? Have you insisted on having your own way? Have you refused to give in even when you knew you were wrong? How far would you go to make peace?

To make peace, one must be willing to give in, to compromise, to come to a mutual agreement. It's interesting that God doesn't give the title "sons of God" to those who make peace but to those who strive to make peace. For it takes *two* willing parties to make peace. All He asks is that you meet a person halfway.

Happiness belongs not only to the peacemakers, but also to the persecuted. If you are persecuted because you have done wrong, you deserve it. But if you are persecuted when you have done no wrong, be happy. All those who want to live godly lives shall suffer persecution (II Timothy 3: 12). If you strive to do your best at everything you do, you can be sure someone is going to persecute you. "What are you trying to prove?" they say. "Quit trying to be perfect!"

In a world where the cry is "Play it cool," mediocrity is supreme. Lying, stealing, cheating are all right if you don't get caught. Loose ethics and morals are the rule. If you "play it straight," you're "out of it."

God knows men so well that He doesn't ask us to do anything without telling us either the punishment for failing to do it, or the reward for doing what He says. In each of the teachings or beatitudes in Matthew 5, God mentions a reward for doing His will.

He tells us we shall be called His children and shall live with Him. What greater incentive could there be to live as Christians?

ASK YOURSELF: Is the prize worth obedience to His will now? Should I let the taunts of men deter me from the prize of the high calling of God in Christ Jesus? Will the Christian life be easy? How often will I fail? To whom will I turn for help?

PRAY ALONE TO GOD.

PRAY ALOUD: Help me to strive for peace among all my friends and neighbors. Let me be good, not proudly but humbly and because of my love for You. Give me strength to endure persecution for Your sake.

Mountain

PICK A SPOT: On a hill or mountain

PICK A LESSON: *Teachings of Jesus, V*

GOD SAYS (Matthew 5: 11, 12): "When you are reviled and persecuted and lied about because you are my followers—wonderful! Be happy about it! Be very glad! for a tremendous reward awaits you up in heaven. And remember, the ancient prophets were persecuted too" (*LB*).

THINK ABOUT THIS: Sitting at Jesus' feet on a hillside must have been a glorious experience. I would have sat there for hours, wouldn't you? These two verses reveal the last of His teachings in Matthew 5. (Perhaps you would like to review the last four days, verses 1-10.)

These instructions to His disciples that day were extremely important. They were the culmination of everything He had said so far.

If you have been a Christian—one born again by the Spirit of God—for a long time, then this advice is especially for you.

If day by day you are seeking to live the Christian life and stay close by the side of Jesus, then be sure that Satan will use every tool to pry you away from the Truth. He even uses other Christians (carnal, backslidden, or Christians in name only) to persecute the true "child of God."

At a recent camping convention, one director said, "Being a real Christian isn't easy! I didn't know what persecution was really like until I became a Christian!" He was referring to the trials that come to someone who is living for Jesus.

At camp, the counselors are always making mistakes, the directors are "bears," the staff people are "grouchy." Just ask the campers! Maybe this is right! And if it is, these people in authority need to get right with God. But maybe the comments come from a disgruntled Christian, one far from God.

If they do, then be happy about it! For God says that you will be talked about and lied about.

People can be cruel—sometimes even people you thought were your friends. They can say all sorts of things about you that you know aren't true. If your heart is right, it will only drive you to your knees in prayer. You will ask, "Why, Lord?" And He will answer, "Because I want to see if you can take it. Trust Me. I will make things turn out right." You will come up from your knees trusting God and asking Him to give you real love for those who have wronged you. He will give you deep peace, knowing that all things are in His hands. You will be comforted to know that other Christians have also been persecuted. What's more, He promises you a tremendous reward because you are able to endure.

ASK YOURSELF: Am I able to take it? Can I really be happy when I am being persecuted for doing what is right? Why does persecution so often come from other "Christians"? Can I have real love for those who hate me?

PRAY ALONE TO GOD.

PRAY ALOUD: God, please give me peace of heart, patience, and a love toward others. May I forgive others when I have been wronged. May I examine myself to see where I might be hurting others. Help me look beyond this life to one of peace and contentment in Your Presence.

Mountain

PICK A SPOT: On a hill or mountain

PICK A LESSON: *Transformation of Jesus*

GOD SAYS (Matthew 17: 1-7): "Six days later Jesus took Peter, James, and his brother John to the top of a high and lonely hill, and as they watched, his appearance changed so that his face shone like the sun and his clothing became dazzling white. Suddenly Moses and Elijah appeared and were talking with him. Peter blurted out, 'Sir, it's wonderful that we can be here! If you want me to, I'll make three shelters, one for you and one for Moses and one for Elijah.' But even as he said it, a bright cloud came over them, and a voice from the cloud said, 'This is my beloved Son, and I am wonderfully pleased with him. Obey him.' At this the disciples fell face downward to the ground, terribly frightened. Jesus came over and touched them. 'Get up,' he said, 'don't be afraid'" (*LB*).

THINK ABOUT THIS: When you've taken a long hike to the top of a high and lonely hill and stood alone in the bright sunshine, what a magnificent feeling overtakes you. It's almost as if you're standing on the top of the world, about ready to reach out and grab the heavens by your hand. God feels so near at this time!

What great joy it must have been to the three disciples that day to be with Jesus in person. How they must have talked about things back home as they walked to the top. Perhaps they became a little weary as they neared the summit of this deserted place. Do you suppose the disciples knew why they were going to the top of the hill?

Can you imagine walking and talking with someone and upon reaching the top, seeing your friend turn into the appearance of an angel? Or what's more seeing two people, long dead, suddenly appear and talk with him?

James and John, brothers, kept quite still when all this began to happen. But not Peter! Dear impetuous Peter, always opening his mouth at the wrong time! Is there one like that among you? Peter blurted out: It's great we can all be here. I'll make three houses. One for you, Lord, one for Moses, and one for Elijah. It took a brilliant cloud and a voice from Heaven to silence him.

Surely He was the Son of God. The God of the universe had spoken and said so. He called Jesus "my beloved Son." He said, "I am wonderfully pleased with Him." To the disciples He said, "Obey Him."

If I had been there that day, I wonder what I would have thought of Jesus' request to keep it all a secret? And what did He mean, "risen from the dead"? Why didn't He just say, "after I am dead"? No other man had ever risen from the grave.

ASK YOURSELF: Why did Jesus have to rise from the dead? Was it for my sins? Will I obey Him as God asks me to? When he asks me to keep secrets, such as the good things I do for others, do I remember to keep still as did James and John? Or do I blurt out everything to make me feel good, like Peter?

PRAY ALONE TO GOD.

PRAY ALOUD: Thank You for the beautiful hills and mountains to stand upon and catch a glimpse of You and Your glory. Thank You for the sunlight and for Jesus to light our every path. Help me to keep the secrets You entrust to me. Help me to obey You each day as I walk the trail of life You have blazed for me.

Life

PICK A TIME: Before breakfast

PICK A LESSON: *Bread of Life*

GOD SAYS (John 6: 32-35): " 'Moses didn't give it to them. My Father did. And now he offers you true Bread from heaven. The true Bread is a Person—the one sent by God from heaven, and he gives life to the world.' 'Sir,' they said, 'give us that bread every day of our lives!' Jesus replied, 'I am the Bread of Life. No one coming to me will ever be hungry again' " (*LB*).

THINK ABOUT THIS: Since breakfast time is near, it's fitting that we should talk about bread and what the Bible means when it calls Jesus the Bread of Life. Bread is one of our staple foods. Each of us eats bread daily in one form or another. It contains many of the nutrients necessary to sustain life (read the label on any package). Prisoners have lived on a bread and water diet for weeks.

Moses and his people in the wilderness received bread from Heaven three times a day. This symbolized that Jesus Christ, the Bread of Life, would come some day, and then people would never again be spiritually hungry.

In the passage just read, the Jews asked Jesus to give them the true bread so they could eat it. They thought it was a special, "enriched" kind of baked bread. But Jesus said, "I am [that] bread. No one coming to me will ever be hungry again." He meant that if they would believe in Him, they would have eternal life.

The Jews began to murmur over his claim to be the Bread from Heaven. Jesus hastened to add that no one can come to Him unless the Father draws him. At the last day all who belong to Him will rise from the dead.

In I Corinthians, Jesus took bread, and when he had given thanks, he broke it and said, "Take this and eat it. This is my body, which is given for you. Do this to remember me" (I Corinthians 11: 24, *LB*). Each church member will recall that this is an important part of the communion service. The bread represents Jesus body which was broken at Calvary for you and me. But He arose from the dead to give eternal life to all those who believe. Surely He is the Bread of Life.

Jesus ends his little sermon to the Jews in the book of John by saying, "I live by the power of the living Father who sent me, and in the same way those who partake of me shall live because of me! I am the true Bread from heaven; and anyone who eats this Bread shall live forever, and not die as your fathers did—though they ate bread from heaven" (vss. 57, 58, *LB*).

ASK YOURSELF: Do I understand what Jesus is saying to me? Have I tasted of the Bread of Heaven? Have I come to Jesus and believed in Him?

PRAY ALONE TO GOD.

PRAY ALOUD: Thank You for sending Jesus Christ to earth to give His Life to redeem me. Draw me nearer Lord, to You. May I partake of You each day as I eat rich spiritual food from the Scriptures. Give me the strength and power that comes from knowing You.

Life

PICK AN OBJECT: Human breath

PICK A LESSON: *Breath of Life*

GOD SAYS (Acts 17: 24, 25): "He made the world and everything in it, and since he is Lord of heaven and earth, he doesn't live in man-made temples; and human hands can't minister to his needs—for he has no needs! He himself gives life and breath to everything, and satisfies every need there is" (*LB*).

THINK ABOUT THIS: How many times have you stepped out into the cold winter morning air and have seen your breath? The warm moisture of your mouth hits the frigid air and a cloud of steam is produced. The other day it was about 97 degrees and I watched a fellow eating an ice cream bar and guess what I saw? You're right! It was his breath. The cold air from his mouth was meeting the hot air of his surroundings. Most of the time, however, our breath is not visible. Because most of the time we breathe in climates closer to the temperature of our bodies.

This breath of ours, indicating life within, was given us by God. God breathed life into the first human being, Adam, and has given it to every human being since then (Genesis 2: 7). Since God gives us the breath that we breathe, He has the power to take it away, and at any time He chooses.

There was a time when God was so disgusted at the evil deeds of men, he almost regretted that He had given man breath. So God sent a great flood to destroy all the people of the earth except a select few who still loved Him (Genesis 6: 17; 7: 22).

Breath is a miraculous thing; it's one thing you can't live without. It is colorless, usually odorless, and contains life-giving oxygen. It's a little like faith in the Spiritual. You can't see it, but you must believe that it is there.

When a First-Aider reaches an unconscious victim, the first thing he checks is his breathing. By placing your cheek near the mouth of the victim, you should feel the warmth of his breath. The pulse and the rise of the chest are other indications that a person is breathing. But if the face looks bluish, you must start artificial respiration immediately. By jutting the jaw, and making a seal with your mouth over that of the victim, you can breathe into him your breath and give oxygen. The body should begin to be warm again, like the child's when Elisha used this method in II Kings 4: 34.

God gave us breath so that we will seek Him and find Him. Breath and health are similar in that we don't appreciate that we have it, until we begin to lose it! The fear that we have when choking on food shows us just how much we value our breath! In a real sense, Heaven or hell is only a breath away!

ASK YOURSELF: Do I stop and thank God often for my breath and my health? I have physical life, but do I have spiritual life? Have I sought God, and found Him? He's only a breath away!

PRAY ALONE TO GOD.

PRAY ALOUD: Thank You for life and good health. Thank You for giving up life and breath on the cross of Calvary for me. May I seek You each day and find You for sweet communion and guidance in every task of life.

Life

PICK AN OBJECT: A pitcher of water

PICK A LESSON: *Water of Life*

GOD SAYS (John 4: 13-15): "Jesus replied that people soon became thirsty again after drinking this water. But the water I give them,' he said, 'becomes a perpetual spring within them, watering them forever with eternal life.' 'Please, sir,' the woman said, 'give me some of that water! Then I'll never be thirsty again and won't have to make this long trip out here every day'" (*LB*).

THINK ABOUT THIS: If each of you would take a glass of water right now from a pitcher or a gulp from a nearby stream, by the time I finish talking you would be thirsty again.

Water has many remarkable qualities. We know that it is composed of two elements, hydrogen and oxygen; it's commonly called by its chemical equation, H_2O. Water is tasteless, odorless, and usually colorless. Scientists say that only when a great density of water is examined does it have its distinctly blue tint. At all temperatures below 32 degrees it is a solid and at all temperatures above 212, it is a gas. It is found in nature in many forms: vapor, dew, frost, rain, hail, and snow, besides the several distinct variations of spring water, well water, river water, surface water, sea water, and so on. It is about the only element of nutrition that man cannot be without for more than three days. It's possible to go without food for much longer than it is to go without water and still live.

Water is necessary for the body to function properly. The majority of our body weight is composed of water. Water has many minerals, but no calories. God puts within each man a clock that tells him when he is thirsty. Whether you follow a forest path, or trek through desert sands, something within you says, "Stop, I'm thirsty."

What an incredible thought that somehow you could have a well of water within the body and never thirst again! The woman at the well, too, was amazed! Her response was what ours would be: "Give me some, right away!"

God offers us Living Water if only we ask Him. He offers us this in the person of the Lord Jesus Christ. God doesn't force Himself or His Son on anyone. We must ask Christ to come into our lives and be that well of water springing up into eternal life.

ASK YOURSELF: Do I have the Living Water in me? Is Jesus Christ my spiritual refreshment day by day? How spiritually thirsty am I?

PRAY ALONE TO GOD.

PRAY ALOUD: Dear God, Fill me full of yourself today. Make my life a well of spiritual water, continually spilling forth your praises to my friends and neighbors.

Life

PICK AN OBJECT: A tree, full of life

PICK A LESSON: *Tree of Life*

GOD SAYS (Proverbs 11: 28-31): "Trust in your money and down you go! Trust in God and flourish as a tree! The fool who provokes his family to anger and resentment will finally have nothing worthwhile left. He shall be the servant of a wiser man. Godly men are growing a tree that bears life-giving fruit, and all who win souls are wise. Even the godly shall be rewarded here on earth; how much more the wicked!" (*LB*).

THINK ABOUT THIS: Have you ever thought of your life as symbolized by a tree? Look at one! See how tall, how straight, how full of life it is! Or can you see one that is black and bare, drying up and dying out?

God speaks of a foolish man and a godly man. *"Timber,"* he shouts to the foolish man. "Can't you see that you're falling . . . down . . . down . . . down! You trust in your money. You continually provoke your wife and children to anger by the things you do. You make your family resent you and hate you. Your money, be it little or much, means nothing to them. Beware! You will always serve another and in the end . . . you'll have nothing left."

"Congratulations!" God shouts to the godly man. You shall have a reward now and in the life to come because you trust completely in Me. Your leaves shall be green (meaning fresh, vibrant, alive) and your fruit shall be life-giving (sharing your love for Christ, winning others for Him). You will flourish as a tree (continually growing in grace and in strength like a giant oak tree).

We should be like a tree of life, with roots deep in God's word—sturdy, not driven to and fro by the wind. Not uprooted by unsound teachings of the world which cause death (Revelation 2: 7).

ASK YOURSELF: How tall and straight am I? What does God require for a truly fruitful life? Can I give life to others before I have it myself? Will I ask God to help me be tall, straight, and sturdy today?

PRAY ALONE TO GOD.

PRAY ALOUD: Help me to be tall and straight like this beautiful tree You have made. May I trust You completely today, and share this rich life in Christ with others.

Life

PICK A SPOT: Near a path

PICK A LESSON: *Path of Life*

GOD SAYS (Psalm 16: 11): "Thou wilt shew me the path of life: in thy presence is fulness of joy; at thy right hand there are pleasures for evermore."

THINK ABOUT THIS: In this psalm, David is talking about the path of life and joy. This is a path that only a Christian can walk down.

Let's think about what a path is. It's a place to walk. It's going somewhere. It makes walking easier. Others have gone before to make the path.

Have you ever walked through a wooded area, or even across a field, where no one has walked before and there was no path? It's very difficult to get through. You might get pricked by thorns and branches or hampered by small trees and tall grass. You have to push your way through and sometimes you get lost.

Think about what a difference it is to walk down a well-trodden path. You know that it will lead somewhere, and no doubt you will get where you're going.

In the same way, a life without Christ, without purpose, is like a wooded area or uncrossed field. The person wanders on through life never knowing just where he is going. He never really accomplishes anything or arrives anywhere. On the other hand, for those who accept Christ, He has prepared a path for them. He says to the Christian, "This is the way I would have you go. Follow me." This path of living is satisfying, enjoyable, and rewarding. This path which God prepares leads to eternal life.

Remember that "there is a way that seemeth right unto a man, but the ways thereof are the ways of death." Jesus said, "I am the way" (John 14: 6). David said, "The Lord knoweth the way of the righteous: but the way of the ungodly shall perish" (Psalm 16). Solomon said, "In all thy ways acknowledge him, and he shall direct thy paths" (Proverbs 3: 6).

Jesus Christ leads down the straight and narrow path that leads to Heaven. Few there be that find it!

ASK YOURSELF: Have I found that path? Do I know the Master Guide who has made that path? Am I following close behind Him? Or am I afar off, straining to see my way?

PRAY ALONE TO GOD.

PRAY ALOUD: Lead me in Your Way everlasting. Make my path straight. Reveal the trail ahead for me day by day as I follow Thee. Keep me by Your side and protect me along life's road.

II
Seed Thoughts

For the Beauty of the Earth

Folliott S. Pierpoint, 1864
Each stanza slightly alt.

DIX 7.7.7. 7.7.7.

Arr. from Conrad Kocher, 1858

1. For the beau-ty of the earth; For the beau-ty of the skies,
2. For the beau-ty of each hour Of the day and of the night,
3. For the joy of hu-man love, Broth-er, sis-ter, par-ent, child,
4. For each per-fect gift of Thine To our race so free-ly given,

For the love which from our birth O-ver and a-round us lies;
Hill and vale, and tree and flower, Sun and moon, and stars of light;
Friends on earth, and friends a-bove, For all gen-tle thoughts and mild;
Gra-ces, hu-man and di-vine, Flowers of earth and buds of heaven;

REFRAIN

Lord of all, to Thee we raise This our hymn of grate-ful praise. A-men.

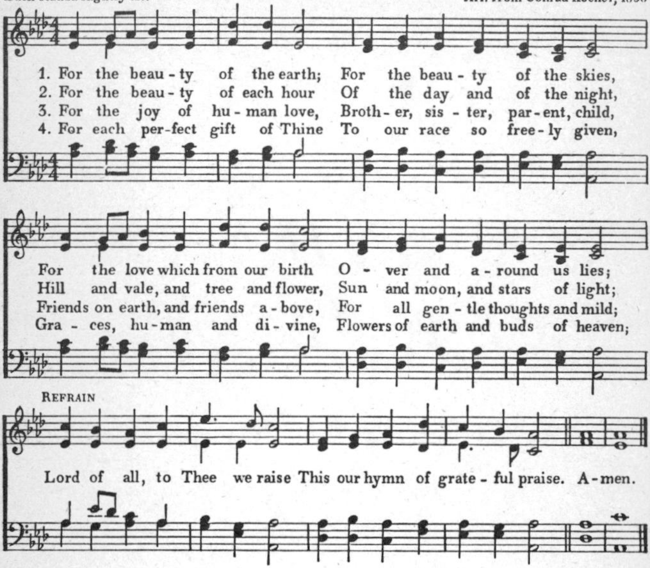

Father, We Thank Thee

Rebecca J. Weston

Daniel Batchellor

1. Fa-ther, we thank Thee for the night, And for the pleas-ant morn-ing light;
2. Help us to do the things we should, To be to oth-ers kind and good;

For rest and food and lov-ing care, And all that makes the world so fair.
In all we do in work or play, To love Thee bet-ter day by day.

Seed thoughts

DEVOTIONAL TALKS are usually improved when a leader offers his own, original ideas. God uses each leader's personality to give His points compelling force. You need only be willing to let the Spirit work in your thoughts, starting of course with the foundation of a passage of Scripture which has devotional potential.

We've chosen a few outdoor topics, and have arranged under each one a list of Bible verses which gave us ideas. Some of them just won't pan out . . . but maybe some of them will act in your imagination, becoming the seeds of effective Christian counsel.

For 40 years in the wilderness, the Hebrews were a nation of campers. They show a deep understanding of the transient nature of life; the Bible often stresses that true security doesn't lie in permanent houses and barns and the wealth of possessions. Each of us must be ready to pull up the stakes and move on, just as Abraham did, "not knowing where he was to go . . . living in tents," which was a mark of his faith (Hebrews 11: 8, 9, RSV).

The Hebrews were closer to the plants and animals of God's creation than most of us are in the twentieth century. When they thought of the objects of daily life, frogs and birds and field lilies came to mind, not TV sets and hamburgers. There are many lessons left for us along the trailside, if we look about us with the help of Scripture.

Suppose you are walking through the woods with a young camper when you spot a frog on a log. Start talking about what it would be like if Cook got to the mess hall one morning and found frogs everywhere he looked. Frogs in the flour and frogs in the oven!

That's what happened to the Egyptians in Exodus 8, isn't it?

In the Bible many references are made to the huts which the children of Israel made out of willow branches and other leafy trees. These were used to sleep in during the feast period. Campers can erect huts on the beach and use them for preparing food for a *luau*.

In the craft shop, many useful items can be made by carving images on pieces of wood. The walls of Solomon's temple had carvings of palm trees, and other nature symbols. If drawing and painting are a camper favorite, try drawing a picture of Proverbs 25: 11 "Timely advice is as lovely as golden apples in a silver basket."

How about starting a collection of small animals, insects, and plants and labeling them with Bible references (or in the case of plants, label them right there on the trail). Some examples:

A grasshopper, with the label, "The Israelites felt this high in the eyes of their enemies." How can a camper resist looking that up in Numbers 13: 33?

A spider: found "in kings' palaces" (Proverbs 30: 28). An ant: "consider her ways, and be wise" (Proverbs 6: 6). A fly: "Dead flies make the perfumer's ointment give off an evil odor" (Ecclesiastes 10: 1, RSV). A bird's nest: the dwelling place of the Kenites is like a nest in a rock (Numbers 24: 21). A snake: the wicked are like poison snakes (Psalm 58: 4).

On a day when horseback riding is on the schedule, select some Bible references about horses and weave them into a devotional talk of 15 minutes or so. You may be surprised at what God has spoken about horses and at how helpful it is. (Read James 3: 2-8 for a start.)

We have listed lots of seed thoughts about animals. But first, let's start with a section of verses which are related to camp life.

Camping

CAMP CONDUCT

VERSES	THOUGHTS
Personal cleanliness	
Malachi 3: 2, 3	The value of strong soap
Jeremiah 2: 22	What soap can't wash off
Isaiah 1: 16	Wash until you're clean
Matthew 6: 17	No excuse for not washing
Deuteronomy 23: 12-14	Camp refuse disposal and latrine duty
Good manners	
Genesis 18: 2; 19: 1	Welcome newcomers to camp
I Peter 3: 8	Let's be one happy family with love and sympathy, courtesy
Proverbs 23: 1, 2	Don't stuff yourself at table
I Corinthians 10: 27	Eat what is on the table, without complaining
Prayer before meals	
Matthew 14: 19; Mark 8: 6	Jesus blessed the food
Acts 27: 35	Paul gave thanks to God
Rest hour	
Isaiah 18: 4	Lord said, I will take my rest
Mark 6: 31	Come aside and rest awhile
Early morning devotions	
Psalm 5: 3	In the morning you hear me
Psalm 88: 13	I pray to thee in the morning
Psalm 59: 16	Sing praises in the morning
Men of God rose early to pray	
Abraham—Genesis 19: 27	Abraham met God early
Jacob—Genesis 28: 18	Jacob rose early to pray
Gideon—Judges 6: 38	Gideon rose up early and prayed
Apostles—Acts 5: 21	Taught in Temple at daybreak
Counselors	
I Chronicles 27: 32, 33	Jonathan was a wise counselor
Mark 15: 43	Joseph, an honorable counselor
Luke 23: 50, 51	A good, righteous counselor
Isaiah 9: 6	Messiah, Wonderful counselor

ANIMALS

VERSES	THOUGHTS
General references	
Genesis 2: 20	Adam named all the animals
Genesis 9: 2	Animals fear man
Genesis 9: 9-11	Covenant to preserve animals
Leviticus 11	Animals fit to eat
Job 39-41	God cares for animals
Ape	
I Kings 10: 22	Gift for King Solomon
Badger (coney)	
Psalm 104: 18	Finds refuge in rocks
Bat	
Deuteronomy 14: 18	Not fit to eat
Bear	
II Samuel 17: 8	King compared to enraged bear
Proverbs 17: 12	Enraged bear preferred to fool
Hosea 13: 8	God's wrath like angry bear
I Samuel 17: 34, 37	God protected David from bear
II Kings 2: 24	Bears bring judgment on boys
Proverbs 28: 15	Wicked ruler like charging bear
Amos 5: 19	Flee lion, meet bear!
Isaiah 59: 11	Complain about lack of justice
Cow, calf	
Hosea 10: 11	Judah, trained for threshing
I Kings 4: 23	Prosperity brings good food
Numbers 19: 1 ff	Red heifer for sacrifice
II Samuel 6: 6	Pulled Ark of the Covenant
Luke 15	Fatted calf for Prodigal Son
Hebrews 9: 12, 19	Sacrificial calf
Luke 13: 15; 14: 5	Water or rescue on Sabbath
Chicken	
I Kings 4: 23	Fatted fowl good to eat
Nehemiah 5: 18	Nehemiah enjoyed chicken
Mark 13: 35	Master's return at cockcrow
Matthew 26: 34ff	Peter denies the Lord
Matthew 23: 37	Like a hen, I would gather you
Deer	
Isaiah 35: 6	Lame shall leap like deer
II Samuel 22: 34	Swiftness and agility
Habakkuk 3: 19	Lord makes me swift like deer
Song of Solomon 2: 9	My beloved is like a deer
Proverbs 5: 19	Ideal wife like a graceful doe
Psalm 42: 1	My soul longs for Thee

Animals

Dog
Exodus 22: 31	Dogs get rejected meat
I Kings	Eat human flesh, lick blood
Proverbs 26: 11; II Peter 2: 22	Fool repeats folly like a dog
Ecclesiastes 9: 4	Living dog better than dead
Job 30: 1	Dogs better than some men
Mark 7: 28	Dogs eat leftover crumbs
Revelation 22: 15	Practice falsehood, like dogs

Fox
Judges 15: 4	Samson uses foxes to destroy
Song of Solomon 2: 15	Foxes spoil blooming vineyards
Matthew 8: 20	Foxes have homes; not Jesus
Luke 13: 32	Herod, a crafty fox

Frog
Exodus 8: 2-14	Plague of frogs everywhere
Psalms 78: 45; 105: 30	God sent frogs to destroy
Revelation 16: 13	Unclean spirits, like frogs

Horse
Genesis 47: 17	Exchange food for horses
Genesis 49: 17	Rider falls off bitten horse
I Kings 10: 25	Horses for gift to king
Deuteronomy 17: 16	Not allowed to breed horses
I Kings 10: 29	Price of horse
Esther 6: 8, 9, 11; 8: 10	Used in king's service
Job 39: 19	Horse's strength from God
Psalm 32: 9	Horse must be controlled
Jeremiah 4: 29	Horses in war
I Kings 4: 26	Solomon's many horses
James 3: 2, 3	Bridle tongue, control body
Revelation 19: 11	Righteous one on white horse

Lizard
Leviticus 11: 29	Considered unclean
Proverbs 30: 28	Even in a king's palace

Mole (mole-rat)
Isaiah 2: 20	Throw away idols to moles

Mouse
Leviticus 11: 29	Considered unclean
Isaiah 66: 17	Punish those who eat it

I Samuel 6: 4	Gold mice as guilt-offering

Mule (donkey)

Genesis 36: 24	Grazing donkeys, find springs
II Kings 5: 17	Mules: beasts of burden
Leviticus 19: 19	Interbreeding forbidden
II Samuel 13: 29	King's sons flee on mules
I Kings 1: 33	Solomon rides David's mule
I Kings 10: 25	Mules given to Solomon
Psalm 32: 9	Mules lack understanding
Esther 8: 10	Messengers ride mules
John 12: 14	Jesus rode on young donkey
II Peter 2: 16	Rebuke from dumb donkey
(Numbers 22: 28)	Donkey rebukes Balaam!

Rabbit

Leviticus 11: 6; Deuteronomy 14: 7	Considered unclean

Snail

Psalm 58: 8	Snails melt into slime

Snake (asp, viper, adder)

Genesis 3: 1-15	Subtly tempted Eve
Genesis 49: 17	Tribe of Dan like serpent
Deuteronomy 32: 24, 33	Poisoned by snakes for sins
Isaiah 11: 8	Child safely plays with snake
Isaiah 65: 25	Dust shall be serpent's food
Ecclesiastes 10: 8	Serpent shall bite you
Psalm 58: 4, 5	Wicked like poisonous snakes
Proverbs 23: 31, 32	Wine is like snake's poison
Proverbs 30: 19	Way of serpent is wonderful
Matthew 7: 10	A serpent instead of a fish?
Matthew 10: 16	Be wise as serpents
Mark 16: 18	Pick up serpents and not die
John 3: 14	Moses lifted serpent; so Jesus
Acts 28: 5	Paul not harmed by snake
I Corinthians 10: 9	Men destroyed by serpents
II Corinthians 11: 3	Be led astray like Eve

Turtle

Leviticus 11: 29	Considered unclean

Wolf

Genesis 49: 27	Wolf devours its prey
Jeremiah 5: 6	Wolf will destroy Israel
Ezekiel 22: 27	Destroy; get dishonest gain
Zephaniah 3: 3	Judges are like wolves
John 10: 12	Wolves scatter sheep

Insects

INSECTS

VERSES	THOUGHTS
Ant	
Proverbs 6: 6-8	Consider the wise ant
Proverbs 30: 24, 25	Small, but exceedingly wise
Bee	
Deuteronomy 1: 44	Amorites chased them like bees
Judges 14	Bees in carcass of lion
Psalm 19: 10	God's laws sweeter than honey
Isaiah 7: 18	Army will swarm like bees
Caterpillar	
1 Kings 8: 37	Plagues—to remind of sin
Psalm 78: 46	Devoured Egyptians' crops
Psalm 105: 34	Destroyed the Egyptians
Jeremiah 51: 27	Horses like a swarm
Joel 1: 4; 2: 25	Destroyed and ate everything
Fly	
Exodus 8: 21-31	Plague on Egyptians
Psalm 105: 31	Swarms of flies
Ecclesiastes 10: 1	Foolishness like dead flies
Grasshopper (locust, cricket)	
Leviticus 11: 22	Fit to eat
Numbers 13: 33	Like grasshoppers to enemy
Deuteronomy 28: 42	Locusts destroy trees, vines
2 Chronicles 7: 13	Locusts devour land
Psalm 109: 23	I am weak as a locust
Proverbs 30: 27	No leader; locusts cooperate
Ecclesiastes 12: 5	Grasshopper is a burden
Isaiah 40: 22	People are like grasshoppers
Nahum 3: 17	Princes like grasshoppers
Matthew 3: 4	John ate locusts
Hornet (wasp)	
Deuteronomy 7: 20	God sends hornets
Joshua 24: 12	Hornets drove out enemy
Louse	
Exodus 8: 16, 17	Plague of lice

Mosquito (gnat)
Matthew 23: 24 — Strain out gnat; eat camel

Moth
Job 4: 19 — Job crushed like a moth
Job 13: 28 — Consumed as motheaten garment
Job 27: 18 — Wicked's house frail as moth
Psalm 39: 11 — Man is frail as breath
Isaiah 50: 9 — Enemies shall be destroyed
Hosea 5: 12 — Ephraim will be destroyed
Matthew 6: 19, 20 — Moths consume earthly riches
James 5: 2 — Garments are motheaten

Scorpion
Deuteronomy 8: 15 — God protected His people
I Kings 12: 11, 14 — Scorpions chastise people
Ezekiel 2: 6 — Do not fear
Luke 10: 19 — Scorpions shall not hurt you
Luke 11: 12 — Give scorpion, or egg?
Revelation 9: 3, 5, 10 — Power of scorpions' sting

Spider
Job 8: 14; 27: 18 — Trust a frail spider's web
Isaiah 59: 5 — Wicked weave spider's web

Worm
Exodus 16: 20, 24 — Worms in food
Deuteronomy 28: 39 — Worms destroy vines
Job 7: 5 — Worms in my flesh
Job 17: 14 — Worm: mother and sister
Job 21: 26; 24: 20 — Men eaten by worms
Job 25: 6 — Man is a worm
Psalm 22: 6 — I am not a man; a worm
Isaiah 14: 11 — Worms are your blanket
Isaiah 41: 14 — Don't be afraid, worm
Isaiah 51: 8 — Worm eats them like wool
Isaiah 66: 24; Mark 9: 44-48 — Worms shall not die
Jonah 4: 7 — Worm attacked plant
Micah 7: 17 — Lowly as worms
Acts 12: 23 — Eaten by worms

PLANTS
VERSES — THOUGHTS

Anise (dill)
Matthew 23: 23 — Pharisees tithe anise

Barley
Exodus 9: 24, 27, 31 — Flax ruined by hail

Plants

Deuteronomy 8: 8	Land full of good things
John 6: 13	Used to make bread
Bean	
II Samuel 17: 27-29	Eaten as vegetable
Bitter herb (dandelion)	
Numbers 9: 11	Eat with unleavened bread
Bramble bush	
Judges 9: 14	Like reigning king
Bulrush (papyrus)	
Exodus 2: 3	Used to make Moses' ark
Cassia (cinnamon)	
Ezekiel 27: 19	Spices sold in market
Cockle	
Job 31: 40	Weed grows instead of barley
Cotton	
Esther 1: 6	Cotton festival-curtains
Cucumber	
Numbers 11: 5	Staple food in Egypt
Flax	
Proverbs 31: 13	Used to make clothes
Gall (opium poppy juice)	
Matthew 27: 34	Offered to Christ on cross
Garlick (garlic)	
Numbers 11: 5	Staple food in Egypt
Gourd (castor oil)	
Jonah 4: 6	Grew to shade Jonah
Hemlock	
Hosea 10: 4	Poisonous plant like judgment
Hyssop	
John 19: 29	Stalk used to hold sponge
Psalm 51: 7	Used for cleansing lepers
Leek	
Numbers 11: 5	Favorite food

Lentil
Genesis 25: 34 — Lentils in Esau's pottage

Lily
Song of Solomon 5: 13 — Lips like lilies

Lily of the field
Matthew 6: 28 (Luke 12: 27) — Lilies neither toil nor spin

Mandrake (like potato)
Genesis 30: 14 — Reuben brought mandrakes

Melon (watermelon)
Numbers 11: 5 — Staple food in Egypt

Mint
Matthew 23: 23 — Pharisees tithe mint

Mustard
Matthew 13: 31 — Small seed grows large

Myrrh (New Testament)
Matthew 2: 11 — Gift to Christ child

Onion
Numbers 11: 5 — Staple food in Egypt

Rie (rye)
Exodus 9: 32 — Not smitten by hail

Rose (narcissus)
Isaiah 35: 1 — Blossoms in wilderness

Rose of Sharon
Song of Solomon 2: 1 — I am a rose of Sharon

Scarlet (like holly tree)
Leviticus 14: 51 — Used in cleansing ritual

Spikenard
Mark 14: 3 — Perfume to anoint Jesus

Sweet cane (sugar cane)
Isaiah 43: 24 — Delicacy prized by Jews

Tare (rye grass)
Matthew 13: 25 — Enemy sows tares among wheat

Thistle
Genesis 3: 17, 18 — Cursed ground
Hosea 10: 8 — Thistles on the altar

Thorn (buckthorn)
Isaiah 7: 23, 24 — Grows thick in last days
Hosea 2: 6 — Hedge of thorns
Proverbs 15: 19 — Thorns in slothful man's way
Mark 15: 15, 17, 18 — Jesus' crown of thorns

Birds

Vine (grape)
Genesis 40: 10 — Rich grapes
Numbers 13: 23-26 — Clusters of grapes to Moses
John 15: 1 — Jesus is true Vine

Water lily
I Kings 7: 19 — Beautifying Temple

Wheat
Genesis 41: 22 — Seven ears on one branch

BIRDS

VERSES	THOUGHTS
General references	
Genesis 1: 20	Birds fly above earth
Genesis 9: 2	Shall fear man
Leviticus 11; Deuteronomy 14	Dietary laws of Israelites
Job 41: 5	Play with him as a bird
Psalm 104: 12	Birds have habitation
Song of Solomon 2: 12	Voice of turtledove
Nest	
Numbers 24: 21	Kenites dwell as nest in rock
Deuteronomy 22: 6, 7	Do not disturb mother
Deuteronomy 32: 11	Eagle stirs its nest
Matthew 8: 20	Birds have nests; not Jesus
Cock (hen)	
Matthew 23: 37	Would gather you as a hen
Matthew 26: 34	Denial before cock crows
Mark 14: 30; John 13: 38	Denial before cock crows
Crane	
Isaiah 38: 14	Clamor like a crane
Jeremiah 8: 7	People of God not like crane
Dove	
Genesis 8: 8-11	Dove finds dry land
Psalm 55: 6	Doves fly away to rest
Psalm 68: 13	Silver wings of dove
Song of Solomon 2: 14, 15	Sweet dove

Song of Solomon 4: 1; 5: 12	Dove, pleasant to behold
Isaiah 59: 11	Doves moan for justice
Isaiah 60: 8	Doves fly like a cloud
Jeremiah 48: 28	Nest in clefts of rock
Ezekiel 7: 16	Doves moan over iniquity
Nahum 2: 7	Doves moan over Nineveh
Matthew 10: 16	Innocent as doves
John 2: 14, 16	Doves sold in Temple

Eagle (vulture)

Deuteronomy 28: 49	Nation as swift as eagles
Job 9: 26; Habakkuk 1: 8	Eagles devour prey
Job 39: 27, 28	Eagles dwell on rocks
Psalm 103: 5	Renewed like eagles
Proverbs 23: 5	Eagle flies toward Heaven
Proverbs 30: 17	Prey on disrespectful children
Proverbs 30: 19	Way of eagle is wonderful
Isaiah 40: 31	Renew strength like eagles
Jeremiah 4: 13	Horses swifter than eagles
Jeremiah 48: 40; 49: 16, 22	Enemy swifter than eagles
Ezekiel 1: 10; 10: 14	Vision: face of an eagle
Ezekiel 17: 3, 7	Great eagle
Daniel 4: 33	Hair as eagles' feathers
Daniel 7: 4	Lion with eagles' wings
Hosea 8: 1	Eagle against Lord's house
Obadiah 4	Soar like an eagle
Micah 1: 16	Bald as eagle for exile
Matthew 24: 28; Luke 17: 37	Eagles gather at carcass
Revelation 4: 7	Beast like flying eagle
Revelation 12: 14	Given two wings of eagle

Hawk (nighthawk)

Job 39: 26	Fly by thy wisdom

Ostrich

Job 39: 13, 14	Has no plumage of love
Isaiah 13: 21; 34: 13	Live in destroyed Babylon
Isaiah 43: 20	Ostriches honor God
Lamentations 4: 3	Women like ostriches
Micah 1: 8	Mournful as an ostrich

Owl

Psalm 102: 6	An owl in the desert
Isaiah 34: 11, 14, 15	Owl shall nest in desert

Partridge (quail)

Exodus 16: 13; Numbers 11: 31	God provided quail
I Samuel 26: 20	David is hunted like quail
Psalm 105: 40	God brought meat
Jeremiah 17: 11	Faithless

Trees

Peacock	
1 Kings 10: 22	Beautiful gifts for king
Pelican	
Psalm 102: 6	A pelican lost in wilderness
Raven	
Genesis 8: 7	Noah sends raven
1 Kings 17: 4-6	God feeds Elijah
Psalm 147: 9	God feeds young ravens
Proverbs 30: 17	Raven punishes disobedience
Song of Solomon 5: 11	The beauty of a raven
Isaiah 34: 11	Destruction of Edom
Luke 12: 24	God cares for His creatures
Sparrow	
Psalm 84: 3; 102: 7	I am like a solitary sparrow
Matthew 10: 29	Though worthless, God cares
Matthew 10: 31; Luke 12: 6, 7	Man more valuable than birds
Stork	
Psalm 104: 17	Stork has a home
Jeremiah 8: 7	Knows seasons; not Israel
Zechariah 5: 9	Vision: wings of a stork
Swallow	
Psalm 84: 3	Swallows have own nest
Isaiah 38: 14	Chatter like a swallow
Jeremiah 8: 7	Knows seasons; not Israel

TREES

VERSES	THOUGHTS
General references	
Isaiah 18: 5	Pruning a tree
Proverbs 11: 28	Righteous flourish like branch
Isaiah 60: 21	Israel, work of God's planting
Daniel 4: 14	Beautiful tree cut down
Hosea 14: 6	Israel will flourish
John 15: 2-6	Pruned branch increases yield
Almond	
Genesis 43: 11	One of best fruits
Exodus 25: 33, 34; 37: 19	Temple bowls like almonds

Numbers 17:8	Aaron's rod yielded almonds
Ecclesiastes 12:5	Almond tree blossoms as usual

Apple

Deuteronomy 32:10; Psalm 17:8	God protected Israel
Proverbs 25:11	Good advice like gold apples
Song of Solomon 2:3	Bridegroom like a fine tree
Song of Solomon 7:8	Bride's breath like apples
Joel 1:12	All good things are gone
Zechariah 2:8	Israel is God's choice

Aspen (willow)

Psalm 137:1, 2	Under willow, mourn for Zion

Box tree

Isaiah 41:19	Planted in the desert

Cedar

Judges 9:15	Fire devours Lebanon cedars
I Kings 7:11	Cedar beams in the Temple
I Chronicles 14:1; 17:1	David lived in cedar house
Psalm 29:5	Power of God's voice
Psalm 92:12	Righteous grow like cedars
Psalms 104:16; 148:9	God cares for His cedars
Song of Solomon 4:11	Pleasant fragrance of cedars
Song of Solomon 5:15	Handsome as cedar trees
Isaiah 37:24; Amos 2:9	Destroyed enemy, like cedars

Chestnut

Genesis 30:37	Used in Jacob's plot
Ezekiel 31:8	Beautiful, but wicked

Cypress

Isaiah 44:14	Used to make idols

Elm

Hosea 4:13	Make shade for sacrifices

Fig

Genesis 3:6, 7	Cannot cover man's sins
Psalm 105:33	God's judgment on Egypt
Proverbs 27:18	Tending a tree brings fruit
Nahum 3:12	Fortresses easily overtaken
Matthew 21; Mark 11, 13	Have faith; don't doubt
James 3:12	Fruit consistent with life
Revelation 6:13	Vision of sixth seal

Fir

II Samuel 6:5	Instruments to praise God
I Kings 5:6	Fir planks in Temple
Psalm 104:17	Provides home for stork

Trees

Song of Solomon 1: 17	Rafters made of fir
Isaiah 37: 24	Wrong attitude; fell firs
Isaiah 41: 19	Planted by hand of God
Isaiah 55: 13	Fir tree instead of thorn
Isaiah 60: 13	Fir beautifies God's sanctuary
Ezekiel 27: 5	Used to build ships
Hosea 14: 8	Fruit comes from God

Hazel

Genesis 30: 37	Used in Jacob's plot

Juniper

I Kings 19: 4, 5	Shade for Elijah
Job 30: 4	Eat roots for meat
Psalm 120: 4	Weapons of the enemy

Locust tree (algum)

Matthew 3: 4	John's food in wilderness

Mulberry

II Samuel 5: 23, 24	God's battle strategy

Myrtle

Nehemiah 8: 15	Used in religious festival
Isaiah 41: 19; 55: 13	Tree as God's sign
Zechariah 1: 8, 10, 12	He stood among the myrtles

Oak

Genesis 35: 4	Idols buried under oak
Genesis 35: 8	Deborah buried under oak
II Samuel 18: 9, 10	Justice by an oak tree
I Kings 13: 14	Man of God under oak tree
Isaiah 1: 30	Wicked like a withering oak
Ezekiel 6: 13; Hosea 4: 13	Offer sacrifices under oak
Amos 2: 9	Destroyed enemy strong as oak
Zechariah 11: 2	Oaks howl at wrath of God

Olive

Genesis 8: 11	Olive leaf, sign of life
Exodus 27: 20	Oil in tabernacle lamps
Deuteronomy 6: 11	Rewards of obedience
Deuteronomy 24: 20	Olives for the widows
Deuteronomy 28: 40	Olives prematurely taken
I Kings 6: 23, 31-33	Ornaments in the Temple

Nehemiah 8: 15	Religious festivals
Psalm 52: 8	Trust God's mercy forever
Hosea 14: 6	Repentant Israel like olive
Zechariah 4: 11-14	Symbols of anointed ones
Romans 11: 17, 24	New branches grafted in
Revelation 11: 4	Olive trees are two prophets

Palm

Exodus 15: 27	Palm trees by water
Leviticus 23: 40	Rejoice before the Lord
Deuteronomy 34: 3	Jericho, city of palm trees
Judges 4: 5	Prophetess dwelt under palm
I Kings 6: 29—7: 36	Palm trees in Temple
Psalm 92: 12	Righteous flourish as palm
Song of Solomon 7: 7, 8	Bride like a palm tree
Ezekiel 40-41	Palm trees posts of Temple
Joel 1: 12	Joy withered as palm tree
John 12: 13	Praised Jesus with palms

Poplar

Genesis 30: 37	Used in Jacob's plot
Hosea 4: 13	Burn incense under poplars

Sycamore

I Kings 10: 27	Abundant sycamore trees
II Chronicles 1: 15; 9: 27	Cedars abundant like sycamore
Psalm 78: 47	Destroyed by God's wrath
Isaiah 9: 10	Sycamores changed into cedars
Amos 7: 14	Gathered sycamore fruit
Luke 19: 4	Climbed tree to see Jesus

Walnut

Song of Solomon 6: 11	Garden of nuts

Willow

Leviticus 23: 40	Build festival booths
Job 40: 22	Willows on stream banks
Psalm 137: 2	Lamenting Babylon exile
Isaiah 15: 7	Flee across brook of willows
Isaiah 44: 4	Israel shall thrive as willows
Ezekiel 17: 5	Seed grows as willow tree

III
Dramatic Devotionals

The Beach

WANT TO TRY something new and completely different? Using the ideas below, relive the experience of the disciples on the beach, that morning when the resurrected Christ came for breakfast.

Or, take the campers to a hillside for a picnic supper, and reenact the feeding of the 5000. Make the Bible a living reality for each young person.

Better yet, select a favorite Bible passage and, using some of the same organizational procedures, write the script for your own devotional drama.

TITLE: *Breakfast Fish Fry on the Beach*
PURPOSE: To experience John 21: 1-14
PREPARATION:

1. Each counselor should read the passage carefully.

2. At morning prayers or prayer meeting the day before the fish fry, ask counselors to pray for the moving of the Holy Spirit in the hearts of campers.

3. At sunup in the morning, send 4-6 male members of the staff to begin fishing from a large rowboat prepared for the "expedition." (Include plenty of fishing gear.)

4. Select at least two people to prepare a large fire (or several small ones) on the beach. (Remember to take safety precautions.)

5. Give the counselors a complete plan for the morning meal, including the skit and its accompanying lesson from the Bible. (This might include a "dress rehearsal" the day before.)

6. When everything is ready on the beach, send a counselor to the assembly area, where the campers will

be participating in morning flag-raising. (Be sure to tell the "officer of the day" to prolong the ceremony until your messenger arrives.)

MENU:
  Tomato juice
  Fish fillet with tartar sauce and lemon wedge
  Toast and jelly
  Milk, coffee, or cocoa

COOK'S PREPARATIONS:

Utensils

  Paper cups and plates
  Napkins
  3 large skillets with spatulas (more or fewer, depending on the size of your group)
  Forks for campers

Food

  Tomato juice (5 oz. for each camper)
  Large (5 gallon) cartons of milk
  Floured or breaded fillets (1 each)
  Bread (2 slices each)
  Melted butter or oil for frying
  Tartar sauce
  Lemon wedges

Start fish frying slowly in skillets, as the beach drama begins. Keep someone near to turn the fillets. Begin pouring the tomato juice and milk or cocoa, using a portable table or the end of an upturned log or two. Toast may also be made and buttered ahead of time (wrap in foil) or it may be handed out to campers to toast over the fire on the end of a stick. (Since the bread toasts quickly, one stick will serve several campers.)

THE PLAN:

Campers should be told that breakfast will be special, and should be invited to bring along their cups for the hot drinks. Or, the breakfast may be a surprise which is announced for the first time at the flag-raising.

As the group leaves on the path to the beach, campers should be asked to walk quietly and in an orderly way. Upon approaching the beach, they should observe in silence what is taking place.

SCRIPT:

Man on beach (*Jesus*): Any fish, boys?

Men in boat: No!

Man on beach: Throw out your net over on the right side of the boat and you'll get plenty of them.

(The men in the boat do as they're instructed, and pull up a [previously loaded] net of fish. It isn't necessary that there be a large number of live fish.)

First man in boat: Why, it's the Lord!

Second man: (Jumps in and swims to shore, pulls net up on shore, then helps the others with any fish they may have.) Why have you come?

Man on beach: Come and have some breakfast, and I'll tell you.

(Invite the campers to join the man and his friends for breakfast. To simulate the Bible event more fully, "Jesus" may hand out the fish and bread to the men from the boat, who will then distribute them to the campers. Following the meal, dispose of trash properly, then ask the campers to remain for a lesson from the Bible.)

BIBLE LESSON:

1. (Read to the campers John 21: 1-14 in *The Living Bible*.) How did John and Peter react to Jesus' presence? How would you have reacted?

2. (Draw word portraits of John, who was closest to Jesus and a patient man, and Peter, who was impetuous and blunt. Show how each reacted in this situation.)

3. (Relate this passage to the Marriage Supper of the Lamb—Matthew 26: 29; Revelation 21: 2—when Christ will again prepare a feast for his beloved.)

4. Whether we realize it or not, Jesus is with us even now, smiling and listening to our happy talk, sharing the thoughts of our hearts. As Matthew 18: 20 promises

us, "Where two or more are gathered together in my name, there am I in the midst of them."

5. (Ask campers to bow their heads and talk to their Lord, telling Him of their love for Him and their desire to fellowship with Him someday in Heaven.) Do you feel close to the Lord right now, able to talk with Him as a friend? If not, perhaps you don't know Him well enough, or love Him fully enough. Each of us should look within himself: Is Jesus my first love? Will I be glad to see His face?

6. Some of you may know in your hearts that you should see a counselor right now, or before the day is over, and get to know Jesus in a real, personal way. Maybe you feel funny about it. But if you take the big step, you'll find there is a great load lifted from you, and a greater love which takes its place. A love for others and for the Bible, the precious Word of God, which you've never felt before.

7. (Dismiss for morning classes.)

Ideas for enriching your devotional time:

Follow up with passages like Matthew 4: 18, 19.

Sing songs during breakfast, such as, "I Will Make You Fishers of Men"; "Let Us Break Bread Together"; "My Lord, What a Morning"; "Put Your Hand in the Hand of the Man of Galilee."

If the lesson is for believers only, put the emphasis on being fishers of men.

The Hillside

TITLE: *Picnic Supper on a Hillside*

PURPOSE: To experience Mark 6: 32-44 (Matthew 14: 13-21; Luke 9: 10-17; John 6: 5-13)

PREPARATION:

1. Ask each counselor to read the passages carefully.
2. Pray. Commit yourselves to God and to His use in reaching each camper.
3. Plan the route for a hike (perhaps around a lake) which will wind up about suppertime near a hillside. (Plan to leave at about three in the afternoon.)
4. At the noon meal, give instructions to the campers concerning:
    a. Proper clothing
    b. Gear (including canteens of fruit punch)
    c. Safety precautions
    d. Organization, procedures
5. Prepare to teach while hiking:
    a. Nature lore
    b. Woodsmanship
    c. How to lay a trail
    d. Collecting for the camp museum

MENU:

Fish sticks (2 for each camper)
Bread and butter (2 slices each)
Carrot and celery sticks
Potato chips
Fresh fruit (apples or peaches)
Drink (provided by campers)

Prepare the fish sticks at the camp kitchen; keep them hot until they're needed. The bread could also be buttered ahead of time. Potato chips are best served right from their bags. Put th... ...it in bushel baskets to carry it to the site. If you ha... them, packets of tartar sauce or ketchup will add to the meal.

PLAN:

1. Campers leave in orderly fashion, with counselors.
2. Camp director and head counselors should leave with the food sometime later. (According to the Gospel of Mark, the disciples went by boat, while the people ran ahead of them to meet them when they arrived. You will be using a boat or a truck.)
3. When the evening meal is set up, ask the campers to sit on the ground in groups.
4. Taking some food in your hand, look upward toward Heaven, and offer thanks.
5. Give the food to your counselors, who will distribute it to the groups.
6. When the meal is nearly finished, counselors should go through the crowd collecting scraps in baskets. (Use bread baskets from the kitchen.) Any refuse should be gathered up by the campers. Then ask everyone to be seated again.

BIBLE LESSON:

1. Read Mark 6: 32-44 (or you may read all the passages).
2. Point out the similarities between what Jesus and His disciples did, and what the camp group has done this afternoon.
3. Ask campers to point out some differences. The main difference, of course, is that in the Gospels the provision of bread and fish was a miracle from the hands of Jesus.
4. Note that only Jesus could perform miracles. His most important was His death and resurrection for our salvation. His body was broken for us on the cross, just as He earlier had broken bread to feed His followers (I Corinthians 11: 24). But now He was providing spiritual bread—manna from God—which gives eternal life to those who receive it.

5. To receive it we must believe. Do you think those 5000 men, plus women and children, believed in Him after seeing the miracle of the loaves and fishes?

6. Tell the story of Thomas, who reached to feel the wounds in Jesus' hands and side, after the resurrection. Jesus said, "You believe because you have seen me. But blessed are those who haven't seen and yet believe."

7. Close in prayer. Give thanks for God's promise of eternal life for those who believe. Pray for those campers who have not yet come to faith.

8. Urge those campers who are unsure to seek out a spiritual person for counseling soon.

9. Still following Mark's account, dismiss the food people first. The leader should remain until the last camper is leaving, then follow the crowd or go by the last boat.

Additional ideas:

Sing hiking songs on the way, or as you arrive: "I've Got Shoes"; "Go, Tell It on the Mountain"; "Hiking Song"; "Tree in the Wood."

You may serve the fish and bread together, from baskets passed among the campers.

You may want to discuss the despair of the disciples at the thought of feeding so many with so little money and food. Certainly it was a lesson in lack of faith. How often our own faith fails!

If you've just finished this book, we think you'll like its companion in the

CHURCH/FAMILY-IN-ACTION SERIES

CAMPFIRE COOKING. Looking for ways to make good-tasting, practical meals a part of your camping ministry? Do you know what utensils, what cooking facilities you'll need, how a family or church group can get the most out of its money and time? Good recipes? The answers are all in this book!
75937—Paperback; 128 pages. $1.95

CAMP DEVOTIONS. The beauties and wonders of nature appear in Jesus' teachings, an appeal that reaches young people especially well today. This guide for the outdoor worshipper helps you pick an appropriate spot, find a devotional text and lesson to match it . . . so you both teach and learn!
75945—Paperback; 128 pages. $1.95

You can order these books from your local bookstore, or from the David C. Cook Publishing Co., Elgin, IL 60120 (in Canada: Weston, Ont. M9L 1T4).

------------------------Use This Coupon-----------------------

Name _____

Address _____

City _____ State _____ Zip Code _____

TITLE	STOCK NO.	PRICE	QTY.	ITEM TOTAL
Campfire Cooking	75937	$1.95		$
Camp Devotions	75945	1.95		

NOTE: On orders placed with David C. Cook Publishing Co., add handling charge of 25¢ for first dollar, plus 5¢ for each additional dollar.

Sub-total $ _____
Handling _____
TOTAL $ _____